Lead Your Oral Litigation

14 Techniques Applied In The Criminal And Civil Areas.

Intended for judges, prosecutors, defense attorneys, litigators, and expert witnesses across all jurisdictions and Spanish-speaking countries.

Deborah Elizabeth Huczek

Table of Contents

OPENING REMARKS

Through this work, I have the great ambition to serve all those colleagues who are part of that minority called LITIGANTS and also those others who soon will be.

When I speak of litigators (men and women), I am referring to those lawyers who leave their mark through their words and actions. That they can be both studious and eloquent at the same time.

A litigator is someone who, despite having been educated in the best universities and knowing the letter of the law, is willing to intervene in a heated dispute in order to win a point in any legal argument.

Litigators are an exclusive category of lawyers who give body, mind, and soul for a noble cause and are willing to fight the fiercest battles in order to find some justice in favor of their clients.

Litigators have a thirst for conquest and go to great lengths to get what they want. Their task is not limited to advising on what the law states, but they specialize in putting the law into action and sometimes into check.

Being a litigator means being willing to go from comfort to discomfort just because you receive a phone call from someone who needs your help. To be a litigator is to honor the profession; it is to do and give beyond the return one can receive.

However, we must be very honest; the profession is highly discredited, and I understand that there are many who have contributed to this.

In my particular case, it was my father who fiercely opposed my going to law school. When he learned of my decision, he became so angry that he stopped speaking to me for a few years.

He told me that this profession was unworthy, that lawyers were dishonest, that they defended criminals, and it was clear that my father did not want that for me.

I will never forget those words, and that is why, in every case in which I practice, I think about how I can bring pride to my parents and to my husband, who, unlike my father, did trust that law was a worthy profession for me.

I must admit, however, that my father had a point.

Over the years, I have discovered that there are colleagues who, instead of defending their clients with the law in hand, use other types of devices or who participate in acts of corruption, who instruct their witnesses to "lie well in court" or who build cases on facts that have never occurred. There are also those who, in spite of collecting their fees, defraud the faith of their clients.

I myself have seen colleagues in the corridors of courts or at the courthouse door teaching their witnesses to lie. Court officials who turn a blind eye to such a daring situation or even tell them: "Counselor, please talk to the witness away from my office door so I don't find out about it."

Clients were evicted because the lawyers did not file the lawsuit, and that led to their rights not having the possibility of being recognized.

There are many examples, and we cannot deny them.

That is why, since I was a student, I have been determined to break down that bad reputation, and by specializing in oral litigation, I felt I had found the way.

I wish, through these pages, to contribute to those main objectives, among which is to elevate the sense of justice of all my colleagues, no matter in which jurisdiction, area, country, or region they practice. I want to provide them with the necessary tools to practice the profession as warriors of the law.

I wish to inspire them to carry forward that renovating impetus, so necessary in these times.

I wish to activate that flame that once awakened your vocation.

Activate the heroic spirit so that you never give up in defense of those ideals that led you to choose this profession as a means of life and service.

In short, I wish you to become a soldier of peace because, through your knowledge and expertise, you can contribute to solving conflicts in a civilized way, avoiding self-righteousness, private revenge, and even war conflicts.

The rule of law and the effectiveness of the fight against any abuse of power depend to a great extent on each one of you.

It is for all this and much more that I wish to contribute and that you contribute in each assigned case to achieve justice for those who need it and seek your help.

I am glad to know that we share this passion and that we are part of the same team.

In recognition of so much sacrifice, hours of grueling study, frustrations, lack of appreciation, and your contribution to this wonderful and challenging profession, this book is written. I hope you enjoy it as much as I did writing it.

Oral litigation

I usually define Oral Litigation as an art that does not give room for improvisation; this has different foundations that we will discover throughout this book.

It is honest to say that the practice of law can be carried out in many ways and through different branches or areas of law; however, the discipline that challenges us the most is oral litigation.

In addition to the technical-theoretical knowledge that is required of us and that we obtained after many years of study, the litigator must incorporate other skills such as strategic case management, team leadership, persuasive public speaking, and effective communication, among many other disciplines.

Oral litigation is the living expression of dynamism and the art of strategy in the pursuit of justice.

Litigation is litigation; it is taking the cases to a decisive instance where, many times, the best one wins and not the one who should be right.

Litigation requires more effort than usual; it is to put into action everything we know, to courageously face the adversary, the system, the representative of justice, and God, if necessary, to defend the rights entrusted to us.

To litigate is to fight in a civilized sense. To fight with words supported by knowledge.

Therefore, as the combatants that we are, our daily work includes effort, demands, and permanent challenges.

We finish one battle and start another, no matter if we won or lost the previous one. We have to train our ability to reinvent ourselves to come back again and again.

This is why a minimal percentage of lawyers engage in litigation in the professional sense of the word.

Many may go to court, taking oral hearings frequently or from time to time. However, few lawyers realize that litigation requires much more than physical presence or last-minute case study.

Litigar is not about experience or years of seniority in the career but about a heroic spirit in favor of justice.

Litigation is the product of a perfect combination of what we know and the thousand ways we find to put law into action.

The meaning of oral litigation from its origins:

Litigation is the scenario where the struggle to resolve is developed; lawyers must orally present their arguments, objections, and evidence in front of a court. For this reason, being involved in the development of oral litigation requires the use of oratory skills and effective communication techniques to convince those who have the ability to make the decision.

Oral litigation has its origins in the cradle of Western civilization. In ancient Greece, the resolutions of legal disputes were made in the so-called forums or public spaces. At that time, the defenses were made orally and were the foundation of its egalitarian legal structure.

This system laid the foundations of law in the Roman Empire and medieval Europe. In England, with the advance of common law, oral litigation took on great importance as an instrument for presenting – before judges and juries – the various legal disputes that arose in society.

During these sessions, the lawyer would excel with a masterful oratory in persuading the members of the court of the merits of his case. This custom influenced the legal systems of many countries that follow the common law tradition.

Today, oral litigation represents the heart of the search for truth and justice in many legal systems.

As it is an act that takes place in real time, it demands dexterity, rhetoric, and a deep understanding of the case by the lawyer. At the same time, it allows the lawyer to integrate non-verbal elements into his or her performance that would never have been possible in written systems, such as voice tones, facial expressions, and body postures, which generates greater emotion and credibility in the presentation of the facts formulated by the litigant. In other words, oral litigation gives a more human perspective to the process.

The vital importance of oral litigation in justice systems

1. Oral litigation plays a central role in judicial systems, providing a complete understanding of the positions in dispute. Oral arguments allow for immediate clarification of the judges' questions, establishing a solid basis for understanding the case.
2. This direct interaction – In addition to ensuring a fair presentation of the matter – fosters transparency, thus building public confidence in the judicial process.
3. In addition, oral litigation acts as a catalyst for lawyers' professional development. By requiring exceptional skills, it drives legal professionals to hone their skills, raising the quality of professional performance, which aids in the better administration of justice.
4. This dynamic approach benefits all parties involved: the lawyers, the assisted parties, the judges, and the public in general, as it contributes to a more efficient and competent judicial system.

In short, oral litigation is a time-honored practice that has evolved throughout history, playing a crucial role in the judicial system. It facilitates the direct presentation of evidence, the immediate evaluation of testimony, and the ability of judges and jurors to interact with the arguments and narrative of the fact in question.

It also provides transparency and speed to the process, as well as the possibility of capturing emotional nuances, which makes it a crucial instrument in the search for truth and the delivery of justice.

Dear Reader

This book, "Lead Your Oral Litigation," has been designed and created especially for lawyers of all levels of experience, as well as judges, prosecutors, defenders, and experts, covering all jurisdictions and countries.

From the outset, this comprehensive guide aims to break the paradigms of teaching in the field of law, as it redefines oral litigation by addressing it with a holistic approach, where the role of the litigant emerges as the architect and conductor of his case and architect of justice. In light of this, I reveal to you the method that I have devised and perfected throughout my experience as a litigator and oral trial teacher. It is a proven method that combines structure, sound leadership, and in-depth knowledge of every technique of oral litigation applicable in criminal, civil, family, or labor law. This will provide you with a complete perspective covering diverse legal situations.

In addition, these techniques, being of international relevance, can be used in the different legal systems of the Western world, allowing litigants to adapt them to their own contexts. On the other hand, they are exemplified with real cases, providing you with concrete examples that will help you understand their application in real-world situations.

Why is this book essential for you?

- You will be able to study in depth 14 substantial techniques of oral litigation with a clear and practical approach.
- You may be a lawyer who wants to strengthen your skills to perform better in court – or to prepare your case from scratch. Perhaps you are a judge looking to improve the dynamics of hearing management within the oral or adversarial system. You may also be a prosecutor who needs to improve the way you argue or, perhaps, an expert witness seeking to present your opinion effectively... In all cases, this book seeks to add value to your performance.
- In addition to offering you timeless techniques or tools, it also provides you with the mindset and tools to quickly adapt to changes in the process and in the legal system.
- Being the product of years of study and dedication to oral litigation, this compendium is backed by real-life experience. As such, you will be learning from real-life cases to understand how to apply these strategies to your cases.

Intended to be more than a book, "Lead Your Oral Litigation" is an indispensable resource for those looking to make a difference in the dynamic field of oral litigation. In other words, for those who want to succeed in their cases.

I know that you will find – in addition to valuable knowledge – Inspiration, help, and guidance on this beautiful path that seeks Truth in attention to Justice and Equity.

- Deborah Elizabeth Huczek

The reason for this book...

Why the DH Method will chart your course to Success in Oral Litigation?

Some comments by the author

When I first attended a courtroom in those years of my journey as an advanced law student, I witnessed (to my painful surprise) a shocking disparity between the conception I had of the processes and the reality experienced in the courts. For, the romantic image - that Hollywood movies planted in our minds - of lawyers immersed in an intellectual confrontation before a judge who resolved the issues raised live, was quickly dispelled. Instead, I found myself in a scriptural system where arguments were set down in documents, signed, and accumulated in files that resembled a bureaucratic mountain more than the judicial dynamics I imagined.

This disconcerting revelation became even more evident when, as a practicing attorney, I participated in hearings in different jurisdictions. Contrary to my expectations, judges rarely took the initiative in these oral hearings. Rather, they became formal and cold - and rather tedious and biased - acts, where questions were decontextualized and aimed only at extracting information that could be inserted into the system. The lack of human connection, disinterest in the search for truth, emotional detachment, and the absence of real dialogue characterized these interactions, even in cases as sensitive as compensation claims for the loss of loved ones.

It was this disenchantment with the system that led me to reflect on the very essence of Justice and the need for change. The dissonance between the exhaustive preparation involved in becoming a lawyer in Latin America and the practical reality of a legal system anchored in formality and obsolescence was unacceptable. It was then that I decided to undertake a search for knowledge beyond the borders of my country.

In line with this determination, I managed to train myself in oral litigation. First, I did it in Argentina through the courses offered by INECIP and, later, abroad, exploring systems such as the Anglo-Saxon and Western systems based on orality. I was the first Argentinean to obtain the title of International Master of Laws with a specialization in Civil and Criminal Oral Litigation. This achievement was the beginning of my commitment to change. This is how my goal crystallized, as I became a transmitter of knowledge and skills, seeking to strengthen the role of my colleagues around the world. With my degree in hand, I returned to my country with the determination to collaborate in the implementation of orality in the legal system and share my experience to inspire other lawyers to lead the change in their respective jurisdictions.

Therefore, my impetus for engaging in oral litigation lies in the conviction that – as executors of the law and active participants in the system – we can not only demand change but also be agents of that change. The comfort of staying within the known rules of the game is an obstacle that we must overcome to achieve more effective, humane, and truth-centered justice.

Specifically, my trajectory as a trainer in Oral Litigation Techniques began with the enthusiasm of receiving proposals to train in prestigious institutes, such as Fundesi (Foundation for Higher Studies and Research), where I discovered that many shared my ambition to change the judicial paradigm. However, I encountered a persistent reality: the resistance to change on the part of the system's operators. In more advanced countries such as Mexico and Chile and in Argentine provinces such as Neuquén, accusatory systems had already been implemented. However, the mere change of structures does not guarantee a real transformation. That is to say, if trial lawyers are not convinced and willing to lead these changes, the vices of the previous system persist; it would be something like changing clothes but not content. Worse still, small advances that we have been making may collapse if we do not act with conviction in their defense.

Towards a transformative justice. The odyssey to change paradigms

One particular episode marked the tipping point that prompted me to transform my approach and contribute to the evolution of the judicial system. The revelation that, despite attempts at reform, entrenched vices persist became the catalyst that defined my commitment to teaching and the search for truth in the judicial process. The "Justice 2020" initiative, a program aimed at implementing orality in civil proceedings, including family and labor, among others, and modifying the Federal Criminal Procedure Code, encountered significant obstacles in its progress. This setback, although discouraging, illustrated the imperative need to overcome reluctance and ingrained inertia in order to achieve a real transformation.

Now, my first shock with judicial reality came in my first hearings, when I discovered that lies had infiltrated the very fabric of the legal system. The telling anecdote – which I continually comment on in my classes, so great was its impact on me – concerns the occasion when at a labor hearing, a forum that should be a bastion of truth and fairness, the hearing lady allowed herself to impart to me an unheard-of piece of advice. In a confidential tone, she assured me that the key to success in cases lay not in the strength of the arguments nor in the strength of the evidence but in the skill of the witnesses to lie most convincingly. In his words, the winners were those who skillfully wove a denser and more seductive cloak of deceit. In the tug-of-war between my reasoned arguments and the shamelessness of these revelations, I clung to the belief that justice should be an unwavering beacon, guiding with its undeniable light of truth. However, my interlocutor insisted that I was living in an ideal, oblivious to the stark reality of trials, which were more inclined toward cunning than righteousness. In other words, the hearing lady, with an extensive background in court, was teaching a novice like me that I had to cheat in the process in order to win. A demoralizing and disturbing message.

The theatricalization of facts, the invention of non-existent situations, and excessive exaggeration were then, and still are, common practices to win cases at the expense of the truth. This phenomenon, together with the lack of effective sanctions against false testimony and false denunciation, procedural malice, and other types of misconduct, became the driving force behind my determination to advocate for the full enforcement of procedural rules and the punishment of the liar.

That is why the essence of my mission takes shape in the fervent support for the implementation -real and ethical- of an oral system, which allows for immediacy and live observation of the parties' expressions. The spontaneity inherent in this approach diminishes the possibility of machinations and fabrications, establishing a more fertile ground for discovering the truth. Having perceived that some lawyers resort to lying due to lack of preparation, I decided to undertake the task of awakening a critical spirit and encouraging reasoning among my colleagues and, of course, training.

The creation of the DH Method to effectively implement oral litigation techniques and provide lawyers with effective and ethical tools to successfully tackle their cases became my contribution to the cause. By sharing this method with my colleagues and other legal practitioners, my goal – in addition to equipping professionals with the necessary skills – is also to foster a new generation of lawyers committed to truth and justice. My conviction is that by changing mindsets and providing rigorous training, we can move closer to the ideal of discovering the truth in the judicial process. This commitment concerns not only lawyers but also judges, who must be equally prepared in these techniques to deliver true, dignified, and honorable justice.

But my goal is also to inspire future generations with ideals that should never have perished. I am determined to change this devalued present. Being a lawyer sounds bad; many interpret it as a profession lacking in ethics, so there are few colleagues who aspire to live with dignity from the profession; they give away their work, and many are those who openly or underhandedly pretend a world without lawyers because, in that way, there would be no one prepared and willing to fight for the rights of others, or warn the failures of the system and to avoid all forms of abuse of power. I want, with my method, to recover that value so that all lawyers who have become litigators can aspire to live comfortably in the profession while serving society.

Personally, I feel that making the defense of others a daily job is a true honor that requires permanent study and commitment. Fortunately, I must say that over the years, I have met admired colleagues who love this profession and act accordingly. Regardless of time limits or the complexity of the cause, they assume their commitment with nobility and determination. This well-deserved recognition goes to all of them.

What was the intrinsic motivation behind the creation of this book?

Well, the reason for this project is my desire, my firm purpose to update and enrich the practical skills in the practice of law. At the intersection of my training and the imperative need to share knowledge, the premise of transcending this training to the collective sphere arose. It is in this context that I asked myself: How to reach a wider audience, transcending borders and sharing essential tools for the practice of law? Convinced that the lawyer is, above all, a communicator invested with the responsibility of simplifying and transmitting the legal corpus, my motivation materialized in the creation of a book that would serve as a means of dissemination on a large scale. Beyond the limitations inherent to the classroom, a book stands as a bridge without borders and without time, capable of reaching diverse individuals and unifying the search for knowledge in a common cause.

This treatise is not limited to the mere teaching of techniques employed in oral litigation but stands as a unique synthesis of my leadership perspective on the legal profession. At its core, it seeks to capture my vision of the lawyer's role in society, highlighting his or her potential as a change agent and community leader. How is this accomplished? The answer lies in the fusion of oral litigation techniques with today's essential elements, such as leadership, personal development, self-knowledge, and the inclusion of ancient Eastern and Western philosophies. More specifically, this book is a study that intertwines the basics of oral litigation with leadership, strategic thinking, research, and storytelling - the DH Method. These skills, far from being ancillary, are presented as essential tools in the contemporary litigator's toolkit. It is not simply a matter of routinely applying a technique; it is about awakening a latent ingenuity, a motivational counselor who guides the litigator toward mastery of the advocacy role.

In essence, this book seeks not only to impart knowledge but to nurture the reader with a novel perspective, merging seemingly disparate disciplines into a coherent whole. It is a call for reflection on the role of the lawyer in society and an invitation to cultivate a more evolved approach. Thus, by the close of these pages, a thorough understanding of the principles and techniques employed in oral litigation will have been assimilated, opening the door to a lawyer who is more complete, more effective, and, above all, more aware of his or her ability to make a significant impact on the administration of justice.

Among the challenges facing lawyers today, it is imperative to highlight the complexity inherent to this noble profession since its inception. A lawyer, in addition to being forced to manage his or her own personal and professional conflicts and challenges, must also assume the task of being the administrator of other people's disputes. In this sense, it is crucial to underline that litigants often become so deeply immersed in the role of representatives that the conflict transitions from being someone else's to becoming their own. This emphasis on being managers of other people's conflicts highlights the need to approach professional challenges holistically. It becomes evident that additional skills need to be included in the lawyer's daily practice. The mechanical application of the law alone is not enough; it is necessary to draw on diverse philosophies and tools to ensure that the lawyer's work achieves its fundamental objective: to obtain justice or solve problems.

Academic training, while essential, cannot ignore the importance of skills such as leadership and personal development. This multidisciplinary approach not only makes the lawyer more flexible but also broadens his or her range of opportunities to address and solve a wide range of legal problems. In the current context, we face additional challenges arising from the automation and depersonalization of legal services. It is argued that artificial intelligence could replace our functions; however, the human essence of understanding others remains irreplaceable. The uniqueness of each lawyer, shaped by his or her life experiences, adds irreplaceable value to the profession. It is vital to convey to the public that lawyers are not simply automatic executors but conflict managers committed to the welfare of people.

There will never be artificial intelligence that can replace the human exercise of our social role.

This is why humanizing the legal profession is one of today's most significant challenges. The depersonalization of service and the possibility of substitution by artificial intelligence require a forceful response. It is crucial to demonstrate that lawyers care about people and seek equitable solutions, not just victory (at any cost). Humanizing justice implies exploring alternative ways beyond prison punishments, prioritizing conflict resolution, and the search for truth.

In the essence of leading a change, courage, self-determination, and a fervent yearning for transformation prevail. It is that everyday life has habituated us to complacency with the status quo, often ignoring the flaws and, more worryingly, even the judges themselves, after participating in my courses, have expressed their disenchantment with a system that they themselves perpetuate. This common pattern, detected during our classroom interactions, reveals the resignation rooted in the perception that justice does not work. I am honored to say that after the classes and the vision I share with them, it is the judges and officials who express relief at finding other ways to manage hearings and administer the justice that is due.

The Impact of the DH Method

Those who have gone through my teaching reveal an inspiring transformation. Some colleagues have shared experiences with me, revealing the palpable pressure and sense of disadvantage when facing these prominent figures in the legal arena. In an environment where reputation can overshadow truth, it is imperative that lesser-known lawyers can emerge not only unscathed but victorious.

Recently, a colleague related to me her encounter with a media lawyer in a particularly challenging case. Although she was initially threatened by the prominence of her opponent, her account reveals a narrative of courage, preparation, and success. This story highlights the importance of the fundamental skills and techniques that we, as lawyers, must have at our disposal to level the playing field.

Facing a media lawyer involves dealing with courtroom situations and, in addition, dealing with the public perception that surrounds these figures. My colleague, in addition to withstanding the pressure, felt confident and up for the challenge. Her confidence was not merely an act of bravado; it was the result of meticulous preparation backed by a well-honed legal toolkit. In the course of the case, this great colleague not only persuaded the judge with solid arguments but also resisted the intimidation that often accompanies media lawyers. Her ability to remain calm and focused on her objective, rather than giving in to diversionary or intimidation tactics, proved to be the key to her success.

The lesson we can take away from this story is clear: it doesn't matter who you are up against in or out of court. Meticulous preparation, mastery of techniques, and self-confidence can level the playing field, even when facing media lawyers. In today's world, where media attention can overshadow the truth, it is essential that lawyers equip themselves with the skills and confidence to face and outperform their counterparts (no matter their media prominence).

Likewise, many colleagues -prosecutors- rely on me to analyze and refine their presentations, ensuring that they are imbued with the essential elements that the DH Method guarantees. The confidence and conviction emanating from the application of these techniques enable prosecutors to face any scenario with confidence and determination.

My teaching method not only provides solid knowledge but also instills confidence through research and a deep understanding of each case. Those who have adopted it have experienced the transformation of their approach from insecurity to conviction and the ability to persuade. It doesn't matter who they confront; what matters is how they confront.

In all of this, in the legal workplace – more specifically in the field of oral litigation – it is imperative to recognize and appreciate the differences that set the tone between an ordinary lawyer and a leading litigator. At the heart of this distinction lies the very essence of strategic planning and the comprehensive vision that, unfortunately, many colleagues fail to embrace.

The lack of meticulous planning leads to blind navigation of the complexities and particularities of the process. It is evident that some practitioners resolve cases on the fly, reacting to procedural steps as they arise. This disjointed approach lacks a methodical and cohesive perspective, and this is where our specific methodology and techniques have proven to be a guiding light for those seeking not only to resolve cases but to do so in an organized and effective manner.

One of the most encouraging observations I have had the opportunity to witness is the transformation in the mindset of many litigators. Our methodology has enabled them to learn to work in an organized manner, set precise goals, and honestly assess whether they are prepared to achieve them. In cases where the answer is no, they have dedicated themselves to training, either in the knowledge of the law, the study of jurisprudence, or even in the development of necessary personal skills. This process of self-evaluation and continuous improvement is essential for professional growth and excellence in legal practice.

But how can the concept of a leading litigator impact the entire career path?

Well, here I want to highlight the direct connection to personal leadership. The leading litigator - apart from effectively guiding his or her cases - unquestionably leads himself or herself. This involves the ability to make informed decisions about the cases he chooses to represent, set clear goals about the kind of lawyer he aspires to be, and consistently communicate the image he wishes to project.

Leadership in the one-on-one customer relationship is equally critical. Showing empathy and leading from a position of equality rather than superiority lays the foundation for strong and lasting relationships. Consistency between who you are and what you communicate creates an authentic and trustworthy image, which is essential to building customer confidence.

Ultimately, leading a case connotes possessing in-depth legal knowledge, but it also entails a commitment to personal development and confidence in ethical decision-making. The leading litigator embarks on a journey of continuous growth, knowing that each choice does not reflect his or her professional competence alone but also manifests his or her commitment to doing the right thing. In this journey, the formation of a coherent image, personal leadership, and excellence in the role of the trial lawyer converge to shape an impactful and rewarding career.

- ***Deborah Elizabeth Huczek***

BUILDING THE LEADING LITIGATOR

YOUR PATH TO PROFESSIONAL SUCCESS!

My method of efficiency in the stages of the process (think, plan, execute)

Being a successful professional means that your client is proud of the lawyer he has chosen to represent his interests and defend his rights, that your adversaries admire you, and that judges respect you.

DH

At another time, one day, when I was finishing my tour in the courthouse, I ran into Juan, a colleague I knew from my university days. We studied some subjects together, and he was a dedicated and outstanding student. That morning, I noticed him distressed and lost; I was worried to see him like that. So, I suggested we had a coffee, and he agreed.

During the conversation, Juan kept repeating, *"I can't understand how I lost this case. It was an easy case, and I felt confident. I handled similar matters and did very well. I can't believe it, what did I do wrong? I don't know what I'm going to tell my client. I have to make something up. I failed him.*

Does this story sound familiar? What happened to Juan back then is part of what happens every day to hundreds of lawyers around the world.

Talking with him, we discovered the reasons for what he experienced as a personal and professional failure; losing an "easy" case is one of the worst *tragedies* that can happen to us, especially if we have "experience" in the field. And I say tragedy because if there is something that identifies us all in this profession, it is the quota of drama that we imprint on life in general.

There are many reasons why a case or many cases -both easy and difficult- may be lost. In spite of having studied all the postgraduate courses and specializations offered to us and even when we are dedicated exclusively to a particular field, these situations are repeated frequently and more than they should be.

The reasons for this outcome are diverse, for example, underestimating the case, not studying enough, excessive self-confidence, believing in the client's story without confronting it with real data, or even suffering from an overwhelming fear of speaking in public. In another order, we could incur underestimating the skills and experiences of our occasional adversary, not paying attention to our skills, and not exercising strategic thinking. All this makes for a "tragic" and "traumatic" experience for us and for the justice our clients seek in entrusting us with the matter. But, unlike what Juan felt and the reflections we made together, it is discouraging to know that many colleagues are not even willing to think about where was the mistake?

The majority tends to blame the client because "he said something he did not have to say," or because "the witness did not answer the questions" or because "the judge is behind in jurisprudence" or because "the adversary colleague had it easy." This does not mean that these circumstances cannot occur simultaneously. However, we can anticipate them, avoid them, or diminish their negative impact if we give the case a leadership vision, which is what I am proposing in this book.

Now, get this! I am not telling you that it is possible to win every case, much less that you can assure the client of an outcome. That would be a serious misconduct. What I am telling you is that only you can avoid feeling like a failure by not doing everything that you should and is required of you.

Because of this and because you are one of those colleagues who are determined to change and steer the course of your legal matters, in the following paragraphs, I will tell you about my method, which I also shared with Juan and many others around the world; it will allow you to work disciplined, focused on long and short term goals, break down mental barriers and, ultimately, reach your goal. This is what I call: "Building the Leading Litigator": your path to professional success!

Well, I don't want the same thing to happen to you that happened to Juan, who, fortunately, and because he learned his lesson, I can say with complete certainty that Juan is not the same as he was that morning I crossed him.

"Building the leading litigator": my method of efficiency in the stages of the process (thinking, planning, executing) through the inclusion of essential skills.

In oral litigation, as in life, it is important to determine where you want to go, to be the master of your destiny, to set specific goals, and to determine the actions you must take within a specific time frame to achieve them. That is why, as part of my philosophy, I have created a series of maxims of oral litigation that allow me to define in one sentence what I want to convey to you.

Oral Litigation Maxim 1: "He triumphs who litigates intentionally."

Intentional litigation is the opposite of improvisation. It requires discipline, commitment, a method, and the development of essential skills that we will be addressing throughout this book, with the intention of introducing you to new ways of practicing law and helping you achieve professional excellence so that you feel gratified in doing so.

But first, I would like to ask you a question that we are often asked in the exams of the subject "duties" or similar, and that addresses the essence of this profession and the way in which we are taught to carry it out:

- Does the law establish an obligation of means or of results? asks the professor.

This seemingly simple question points to a fundamental issue. Lawyering, as the codes and university lessons teach us, is a service. Therefore, we cannot guarantee results or assert to the client that we will successfully resolve his or her matter. To do so could have consequences.

However, behind this premise, there is another message that, in my opinion, has harmed our profession and is reflected in how society perceives us.

Many lawyers work; some warn others are more automated, with no intention of getting anywhere, as mere managers who perform actions disconnected from each other, and when the result arrives (unpredictable for many), they respond that is how it is: justice works poorly and a series of excuses, which is not relevant to the list because they are endless.

This is because we have fallen into the trap of confusing the impossibility of guaranteeing results with the idea that we cannot work to obtain them. Herein lies the main problem: on many occasions, we work without a clear purpose, without questioning the fundamentals of this profession. How can we work towards success, the one I spoke about at the beginning, through strategic litigation?

Lucius Annaeus Seneca rightly stated that "there is no favorable wind for those who do not know where they are going." It is necessary to litigate intentionally, to direct all our actions and thoughts towards a clear objective. Strategic litigation, especially in the oral arena, is governed by two fundamental maxims: litigation is an art, and justice is closer if lawyers are well prepared.

My interpellation is that you stop working and litigating without looking for your reasons, that you start working with specific objectives and establish actions to achieve them.

As a result, case preparation and strategic litigation are crucial.

It is about developing skills such as leadership, research, strategic thinking, negotiation skills, and narrative ability. Leadership, exercised both with the work team and in front of the judge and the client, is essential to lead the case, deal with conflicts in a creative way, and represent values.

These skills are fundamental to direct the case towards success, with a clear purpose guiding all our actions throughout the judicial process.

Let's take a look at each of them below.

➢ Leading Lawyer

Leadership skills are essential for any lawyer who wishes to lead his or her team and plan their case effectively. Leadership involves the ability to inspire and guide others in the pursuit of shared values and goals.

Therefore, it is essential that you work on developing leadership skills in four key areas: your relationship with yourself, your relationship with the client, the management of your team, and your role as a lead attorney in representing the case before the judge or jury.

Lawyer and his path to self-leadership development

In the first place, knowing that the unfolding of human potential starts from a base: the relationship that the individual establishes with himself, it is of vital importance that the lawyer who wishes to perform effectively and efficiently works on his self-concept, practicing the inner dialogue in an honest way for good self-knowledge. In order to be able to identify his strengths and work on transforming his limitations through the development of skills, Leadership should not only be applied in work situations or with respect to your teams but also in your personal life. The leadership that should be exercised over oneself focuses on being the owner of your actions, thoughts, and emotions. In other words, it is the ability to make decisions with intention and to stay focused on your goals and values.

One of the keys to leading yourself is self-knowledge. Knowing your strengths, weaknesses, values, and goals will allow you to make better decisions and be focused on what really matters; for example, find the necessary tools to make up for or solve those weaknesses and develop dormant skills. It is necessary to accomplish the effective task of improving yourself in favor of your objectives.

Likewise, it is essential to be aware of your thoughts and emotions so that you can manage them effectively and not let them affect you negatively.

Another important key to leading yourself is discipline. Discipline involves setting clear goals and constantly working to achieve them, even when you don't feel motivated. It means having the commitment and perseverance to carry out the actions necessary to achieve your goals and not allowing distractions or lack of motivation to throw you off track.

At the same time, it is essential to cultivate an enthusiastic attitude and renewed faith, which will allow you to maintain an optimistic outlook even in difficult situations, helping you to overcome obstacles and find creative solutions. On the other hand, responsibility implies assuming the risk of your actions and decisions and not blaming others or external circumstances for the results.

Leading lawyer in relation to his client or represented party

Mutual respect and transparent communication are essential in the relationship between a lawyer and his client. In my experience as an oral trial teacher, I have always taught my students that the lawyer and client form an indivisible working team and that the lawyer should not consider himself superior to the client because he has more legal knowledge. In fact, undervaluing the participation of a client who needs collaboration can be counterproductive.

To establish a relationship of trust, the attorney must be honest and transparent with the client, explaining the weaknesses of the case, the evidence needed, and the strategy to be used. In addition, it is important for the attorney to inquire about the client's life history in order to tailor the theory of the case and present it in a coherent manner before the hearing.

As lawyers, we are stewards of others' interests, which means that we represent others and defend their rights. It is, therefore, essential that the client feels well-represented and proud that he or she has chosen the right lawyer for his or her case.

Leading lawyer in relation to his work team

Third, it is important to note that the exercise of leadership within a team is essential. Although some litigators work without collaborators, in certain circumstances, they may need the help of other experts with more experience in the subject matter. In such cases, it is crucial that the team be motivated and inspired by the leader.

First, the leader must be able to generate genuine interest in the team about the rights involved in the case, its history, and everything related to it. A collaborative approach using brainstorming and conversations in an open and free environment can enrich the case by finding new solutions or legal defenses. It is in this context that the hypothesis and what would be the best thesis to defend at trial should be discussed with the team.

In addition, the correct distribution of roles and the sum of individual efforts under the correct direction of the leader can lead to the gathering of valuable information about the case and its participants.

During this relationship, the litigation leader must be a role model, reflect the values he or she espouses, and inspire team members to do the right thing. A good leader is one who assumes the risks of poor management and who also recognizes in each of his collaborators the importance of their contribution and how they have contributed to obtaining the desired result.

The teamwork mentality is rare in this profession and needs to be developed.

Leading counsel in relation to third-party decision-makers

Finally, we will address the issue of the attorney's leadership in presenting the case to an impartial third party, such as the judge or jury.

As a team leader, the lawyer is charged with representing the case before the judge adequately and convincingly, to the best of his or her ability. This involves the ability to persuasively and consistently communicate the arguments and evidence in the case and to respond to questions and objections appropriately.

Also, integrity, responsibility, and seriousness are crucial qualities that the lawyer must demonstrate at all times during the trial since their credibility is the best tool to gain the confidence of the jurors or the judge. Once the thesis has been established through work on the theory of the case, the attorney must lead the presentation of the case passionately.

It is important for the lawyer to consider at the outset how he will conclude his presentation and what words he will use to do so. The closing argument is a critical opportunity to bring all the elements of the theory of the case together in front of the judge and convince him of the validity of his argument.

The authenticity, conviction, and determination of the litigant will make the difference in defending oral arguments.

Leading then means demonstrating that we have done a good job and that we are in a position to defend it despite the onslaught of the adversary.

➢ Lawyer Strategist

Maxims of oral litigation 2: "Litigation is an art that gives no room for improvisation."

The spontaneity of oral hearings, in that heated mano-a-mano between adversaries and between adversaries and judges, makes it impossible for us to have enough time to think carefully about how we should respond to each dispute or request. It is now already that an adequate argumentation or response is demanded of us. Therefore, only those who know their case deeply, have their objectives in mind, and are willing to follow the plan will have the best mental agility to respond to these challenges.

A litigation strategist is a litigator who looks beyond the trial and draws a comprehensive plan that includes all stages of the process (pre-trial, oral, and appellate) in its analysis and only then makes decisions.

This second essential competency or skill that the trial lawyer must cultivate is mastery of strategy.

A term borrowed from military conflicts that, when applied to oral litigation, involves us in a very particular way since we are required, after analyzing all the conditions surrounding the event, at least those known up to that moment, to design a plan with short, medium and long term objectives.

This, in turn, involves the possibility of reaching early solutions to the conflict, such as the application of alternative measures, negotiation, and mediation, as well as the filing of nullities or exceptions, the behavior we assume in and out of court, as well as a detailed analysis of how our decisions may benefit or harm those involved in the present dispute.

If that were not enough, it is necessary to analyze the potential strategy of the adversary, thinking that he could be successful. Only in this way will we be able to anticipate the opponent's move in order to give him a quick counterattack.

Within this analysis, we must also include a special section that involves the tendency of the court in similar cases, what evidence I will be able to obtain, what its possible result is, and what difficulties you will have to face.

The litigator in the adversarial system or in oral hearings must not only be prepared to respond boldly to interpellations from opponents and judges but must also learn to weave astute strategies early on. From the investigation phase to the oral defense in court, the lawyer's ability to anticipate moves, evaluate evidence, and build solid arguments is critical to success in the defense or prosecution.

Why is this skill imperative?

First, similar to the comprehensive planning and design of a house by an architect, the lawyer strategist must conceive his or her work holistically, from design to execution. Starting with a solid work plan and executing it meticulously at every stage of the process is imperative.

This planned approach requires the attorney to chart a clear path, thoroughly understand the starting point and ultimate goal of the case, as well as to anticipate and investigate potential setbacks and surprises throughout the trial.

Therefore, deviating from this meticulously planned route could compromise the strategy, generating an adverse impact on both the client and the representation of the case.

Preventive work not only reveals potential weaknesses that lawyers must address, whether in terms of their own professional skills, the case, the client, and the narrative to be presented at trial, but also demonstrates consistency, firmness in values, and a clear understanding of objectives.

In fact, when working with a team, this strategic approach allows you to lead. It is a demonstration of conscious direction, where the lawyer not only understands where he or she is going but also knows how to get there. It is a matter of delimiting the work, establishing final goals, and determining, through an action plan, how each of these objectives will be achieved.

Next, key activities are identified, secondary tasks are organized for efficient implementation in a second stage, and the information needed to complete and adequately represent the case at trial is evaluated. This method provides a solid structure for organizing available information and identifying gaps that need to be filled for an effective presentation in court. Thus, the trial lawyer's strategic ability is not only a tool for his or her own success but also the compass to guide his or her team towards the achievement of solid and well-founded objectives.

➢ **Investigating attorney**

Oral Litigation Maxim 3: "At trial, I am not going to investigate what happened; I am going to prove it."

Curiosity, wanting to get an answer from a reluctant witness, not knowing the outcome of an investigation, or not understanding it because of its complexity can really ruin your case. Let's see how developing this skill can save you from making serious mistakes in the process.

In the contemporary 21st century, under the prevailing oral system, the trial lawyer cannot merely rely on the comfort of his office, passively waiting for information to arrive. This professional, who faces oral hearings in a mano-a-mano with his adversary, does not have time to go looking for information in books, not even in his own notes. He must be ready to respond to every onslaught, which can be achieved when he has done a thorough investigation of the case to such an extent that he can synthesize complex information using simple words.

The investigative litigator assumes the challenge of gathering exhaustive information, surpassing even his defendant's knowledge of the facts involving him. Therefore, it is imperative for the attorney to develop independent investigative skills without ignoring the possibility of collaborating with private investigators or experts.

Legal research goes beyond mere file review; it involves active immersion in the facts. The attorney, leaving the comfort of his or her office, ventures to the scene of events, interviewing witnesses, exploring crime scenes, and gathering data that is not always reflected in the file.

It is essential that this inquiry be conducted in an objective manner, allowing counsel to expand on the information in the file and to discern what to present and what to reserve. In an oral system, where the relevance of the trial lies in the determination of the facts, counsel must undertake all actions conducive to discovering the truth.

The attorney-investigator, after gathering information, forms a conviction different from the one obtained only by reading a file. This process allows him/her to determine the evidence necessary to prove the facts of the case in an oral trial, consulting other professionals depending on the matter.

Role of the lawyer as investigator

1. **Interviews and data collection:**

- Go to the scene to confirm or discuss the circumstances surrounding the situation.
- Obtain valuable information not provided by the assisted persons or reflected in testimonies or records.
- Collect information through filming, photographs, sketches, and interviews with neighbors.

2. **Customer research:**

- Inquire about the client's reputation in the area, professional background, and family relationships.
- Evaluate the suitability of the witnesses proposed by the client to avoid surprises during the trial.

3. **Witness analysis and perception conditions:**

- Probe into the life of the witnesses, their relationship with the client, and the parties involved.
- Identify the conditions under which the witnesses are perceived, such as their working hours, personal relationships, etc.
- Evaluate the usefulness of witnesses and anticipate weaknesses that may arise at trial.

This procedure will strengthen the lawyer's position as the most informed insider in the case and will certainly provide the tools to strategically anticipate and counter the opponent's arguments. Thorough investigation, in the hands of a committed lawyer, becomes an essential pillar in revealing the truth and prevailing in the oral system.

➢ **Storytelling lawyer**

Oral litigation maxim 4: "The better the evidence, the more persuasive the story."

The trial is not a game; therefore, it is not a matter of arguing about unproven facts, distorting the result of the evidence, theatricalizing invented facts, or exaggerating their significance. Therefore, the litigant who has demonstrated throughout the trial that the facts have occurred in the manner in which he anticipated them would be in a better position to win because this has been proven.

Let's see how this skill can enrich and enhance your oral presentations:

Once the litigator has selected the thesis he will defend at trial, he embarks on the crucial task of developing the narrative of his case, akin to writing a novel.

This phase involves the careful integration of the protagonists, the exposition of the conflict in question, and the detailed unfolding of the investigation, unraveling key aspects such as the scene of the event, the underlying motives, and the concomitant events surrounding the event.

At this point, through persuasive storytelling, the litigator must address universal concerns, answer latent questions, and lead listeners to the conclusion of the plot by revealing the substance and deeper meaning of the events. This value, discovered in the process of developing the theory of the case, must permeate every word expressed during the oral presentation.

The adoption of this narrative skill goes beyond mere litigation; it becomes an instrument to bring justice closer to the public sphere. It allows the figure represented in the trial, far from being pigeonholed in simplistic labels, to be revealed in all its complexity and humanity.

The goal is clear: to get jurors to become immersed in and identify with our version of the facts, creating an emotional connection and a deep understanding that transcends the confines of legal argument.

Infographic: Building the Leading Litigator

Leading Lawyer Skills

Competition	Description
Leading Lawyer	➔ *Leadership development in four key areas: self-concept, customer relationship, team management and room leadership.* ➔ *Self-leadership: inner dialogue, self-knowledge, discipline, positive attitude, and personal responsibility.*
Leading client relationship lawyer	➔ *Mutual respect and transparent communication.* ➔ *Formation of a team to work with the client.* ➔ *Honesty about case weaknesses and strategy.* ➔ *In-depth knowledge of the client's life history to tailor the case theory.*
Leading attorney in relation to his work team	➔ *Inspire interest in the rights and history of the case.* ➔ *Active collaboration with the team: brainstorming, hypothesis, and thesis discussion.* ➔ *Motivation of the team through shared values.*
Leading counsel in relation to third-party decision-makers	➔ *Persuasive and coherent representation of the case before judges and juries.* ➔ *Integrity, responsibility, and reliability as crucial tools.* ➔ *Careful preparation for the presentation of the case at trial.* ➔ *Closing argument as a decisive opportunity to consolidate the theory of the case.*

Skills of the Lawyer Strategist

Competition	Description
Lawyer Strategist	➔ *Holistic case planning: design, execution, and anticipation of mishaps.* ➔ *Preventive work to identify weaknesses and consistency in presentation.* ➔ *Evaluation of information necessary for the presentation at the oral trial.* ➔ *Identification of key activities.* ➔ *Organization of secondary tasks.*
Team Strategist Lawyer	➔ *Strategic leadership to guide the team towards a solid goal.* ➔ *Delimitation of goals and action plan to achieve the objectives.*

Skills of the Investigating Attorney

Competition	Description
Investigating attorney	➔ *Development of independent research skills.* ➔ *Collaboration with private investigators or experts.*
Role of the lawyer as investigator	➔ *On-scene interviews and data collection. Client investigation and witness evaluation.*

	→ *Analysis of conditions of perception and relevance of information.*

Storytelling Lawyer Skills

Competition	Description
Storytelling lawyer	→ *Development of the narrative of the case with the integration of protagonists, details of the conflict, and details of the investigation.* → *Persuasive answers to universal questions.* → *Creating emotional connection and deep understanding.*

If you have arrived here, you have taken a step towards transforming your reality and becoming a valuable litigator and leader in your field.

From now on, we will fully enter into the techniques that make up the art of oral litigation. And it should be said, too, that I have already prepared your mind to approach more boldly and unequivocally these important tools of legal practice that you will encounter throughout this book.

This is just the beginning of a fruitful journey on your way to professional success, so don't stop.

THE IMPORTANCE OF FAIR PLAY IN THE ADVERSARIAL PROCESS

"The litigant shall act in accordance with the constitutional principles and require that the authorities and so does your adversary."

DH

Lawyers also work on Sundays.

The story I share with you below probably sounds familiar to you. Surely, you have been called to provide your services when you were celebrating a birthday, playing with your children, or maybe in the middle of a date. Duty calls at unexpected times, and you have to put on your suit and go out to do battle.

...Sunday had finally arrived; it was necessary to take a break and distract my mind after a hectic week of hearings, new cases, courses, exams, and my family worries. We were ready: my husband, my 4 children, and I to go out to celebrate a friend's birthday at his weekend house. The plan sounded really fascinating. Spending time with family and friends was just what I needed. But... suddenly, the cell phone rang. On the other end of the phone, I could hear an anguished woman, who, in a very disorganized way, was telling me about her husband's arrest and asking me to quickly come to his aid, for which she would have to travel more than an hour. From the many questions I asked Roxana, I managed to understand that the police had been at the family's supermarket for two hours, saying that they were there because they had received a complaint. They demanded her husband to show the purchase invoices of some alcoholic beverages, to end with the seizure of some merchandise and the arrest of those who would later be my clients.

So, after agreeing on a fee, we suspended our plans, and I asked my husband to take me to the police station while I arranged for friends to take our children to the party.

I went to the police station, where I was informed that my clients had been transferred to a prosecutor's office in the Province of Buenos Aires. I was really surprised by the speed with which they were moving in this "very particular" case. We set off again, and when we arrived at the Prosecutor's Office, I presented myself as a lawyer at the front desk, asking to know the reasons for the detention, the crime for which they were accused, and, of course, to be allowed access to the file. In addition, I wanted to have a direct interview with my clients. All the aforementioned usually do not present great difficulties or should not present them; however, in this case, everything indicated that it was not going to be the same.

The instructor, in principle, told me that they had already accepted the intervention of the official defender, that they were soon going to testify, and that, for that reason, it was not necessary for me to be there. The situation was getting complicated, and there were no reasons or, at least so far, I was not aware of them. My suspicions increased when they did not want to give me information about the case or receive my presentation. In response to my insistent reply, they told me that... "*The accusation, the instructor stammered, was for smuggling and theft of merchandise in town and in gangs.*" This was a contradictory accusation, but it could not be possible because my clients were merchants, not thieves or asphalt pirates.

Then, I began to wonder what was behind this detention. How was it possible that it was the Prosecutor's Office that denied them the right to assign a lawyer they trusted and that I was denied the right to fulfill my duty to represent them? The previous experience made me wonder: *Why did the official want to rush the statements of the accused? Why were they transferred so quickly? And why was I being excluded?* These were some of the questions I asked myself while I demanded the presence of the head of the Public Prosecutor's Office. Then, I went to the Court of Guarantees on duty to inform the judge of the irregularities that were being committed, both in writing and with my arguments expressed out loud. I was ready for anything; I had to make myself heard, and there was no other choice. I requested, energetically, that I be allowed -immediately- to have direct contact with my clients and to enter the file in full. And finally, my request was granted.

After overcoming all these obstacles and quickly reading the file, my suspicions were confirmed. The detention could never have been carried out; therefore, it was illegal and was based on a totally irregular procedure. My clients had suffered serious violations of their constitutional guarantees, and I had to expose them. Of course, I began to outline a defense strategy that consisted, in the first place, of requesting the decree of nullity of the police procedure as well as of the illegal detention suffered by my clients.

That is to say; I had to attack from technical and procedural issues the police action that had so far been hastily validated by the prosecution, in addition to demanding energetically and immediately that my defendants be brought in for this interview, which the prosecution wanted to avoid.

All of this did not go down well with the instructor who, like me, was working on a Sunday and was in a hurry to resolve the case until this private attorney arrived with these and so many others that, for didactic purposes, we will leave for another occasion.

It is important to remember that, for some officials, private attorneys can be a hindrance, as we demonstrate that our commitment is to our client and that we are therefore determined to control every act and to defend the validity of the guarantees and rights at stake in each case.

However, what some officials think about our role should not affect the actions we must take, especially when arbitrary acts such as the one described above are committed.

In short, what I want to convey, using this case as an example, is that we litigants must safeguard -at all times and places- the constitutional guarantees of our clients, not only in the middle of the oral trial but also as in this case, in the initial stages of the process. These violations can be committed by officers of the security forces, as well as by judicial officials and the person in charge of the investigation. Consequently, we lawyers must be prepared to stand out even on a Sunday, with the process underway and our clients arbitrarily detained. We must be ready because when duty calls, there is no time to pick up our books and start studying.

It is you, a lawyer, private litigant, or public defender, who must be willing to go through moments of discomfort and defend the rights entrusted to you. Because, in the end, "Each and every one of us, litigators around the world, have taken the same oath: to defend the validity of individual guarantees that are affected. Therefore, we must honor that promise with concrete acts, right words, and solid arguments every time it is necessary, and duty calls us in front of whomever."

The oral process: Essence of the adversarial process

The litigator stands heroically in defense of the laws and the system against any abuse of power.

The adversarial process model stands out as a substantial innovation in comparison with other procedural systems. It represents a revolutionary approach to the trial process, marking a clear break with previous practices, especially the inquisitorial and mixed process. In this way, it stands with the mission of safeguarding individual guarantees and citizens' rights, establishing crucial rules and principles that every legal professional must understand and apply to ensure compliance with due process.

However, the implementation of the accusatory process does not guarantee its full operation and effectiveness. To achieve this, it requires will, determination, constant training of its operators, commitment of the entire legal community, control, and follow-up by the authorities, among others.

But more important than all of the above is the role that litigants play both inside and outside the process since we are the ones who detect those flaws that openly or covertly damage everything that has been achieved.

Observation of reality shows that, although we have made progress both in the transparency of the systems and in their efficiency, we still have a long way to go. We cannot assure that these advances are consolidated; on the contrary, the oral system and its principles frequently suffer attempts at destabilization.

It must be recognized that there are always attacks on this type of process because many do not find it convenient. Attacks can be generated from within, either by operators who have an inquisitorial mentality, because they are not prepared in strategic litigation techniques, or because they do not respect the guarantee of fair play. Attacks can be exercised by the security forces by advancing against individuals because they do not find a brake in the judiciary. The onslaught can be exercised by any power of the state because the system of checks and balances does not work. Also, those that come from the press or other apparatuses of power by not respecting the procedural rules established for the clarification of the facts.

That is why I have full confidence in the social role played by trial lawyers. We are the ones who, unaware of the numbness or habit of belonging to any branch of government, can give an early warning that something is wrong and act accordingly.

It is we who must be attentive and react. In times when many want to discredit us or impose the idea that we are expendable, it is necessary to respond with greater force. It is we, the litigants, who report the commission of violations of life, liberty, security, and so many other goods and rights at stake. Thanks to us, these transgressions are not the rule but the exception. Thanks to us, the belief that justice can be achieved is a reality.

My call is open and clear: I want you to feel and become a hero since that is how we are perceived by those who suffer an undeserved situation and come to our aid.

Because all of us lawyers are obliged to act in defense of the supreme law. We are often perceived as the hero who rescues the unjustly detained, who is willing to fight with bold arguments against authority, and who confronts face-to-face the aggressor of a hopeless victim. We are the intellectual warriors dressed in suits or heels, who, with the National Constitution in hand, go out in the mornings to litigate so that our clients receive the relief they demand. We are the ones who collaborate in the search for truth and make our countries fairer places. Our task is noble and fundamental; therefore, we should exercise it with great pride.

Analysis of the adversarial process

An approach focused on truth, justice, and the protection of the individual.

Because...Changing costumes does not mean changing content.

Despite the appearance of remoteness that this discussion may have on the differences between an inquisitorial, mixed, or adversarial process, it is crucial to remember that the inquisitorial system was in force throughout Latin America until very recently and even in some jurisdictions of Argentina, where I practice, it continues to be applied at the national level for the investigation of major crimes. It is only now that the new Federal Criminal Procedure Code, based on an accusatory approach, is being implemented.

It must be said that the inquisitorial procedure is not a relic forgotten in time but rather an entity whose foundations are worthy of being remembered and analyzed. The preeminent characteristic of this process lies in the consolidation of powers in the hands of the judge, who held exclusive authority to prosecute, investigate, and punish the accused for a specific crime. The inquisitorial judge, vested with the authority to initiate investigations ex officio, exercised, through the attributes conferred by his investiture, various actions aimed at clarifying the commission of an alleged crime.

However, it is sincere on my part to recognize that this inquisitorial profile can be present even within an accusatorial process and that I have had to deal with prosecutors who are more inquisitorial than the former judges who exercise or exercised in an inquisitorial or mixed system. We can also see its characteristic features in civil, family, or contentious administrative proceedings.

However, it is essential to emphasize that, in addition to leading the investigation, the inquisitorial judge assumed the responsibility of pronouncing sentences and sentencing the suspect for the facts he himself had investigated. This confluence of jurisdictional and accusatory powers in a single figure was possible thanks to the conception of the judge as a divine delegate, whose powers emanated from the monarch, in turn invested as God's representative. The powers conferred by the king were perceived as a divine delegation, attributing to the judge certain virtues and special gifts that differentiated him from ordinary citizens.

In the context of this inquisitorial system, the judge's rulings enjoyed absolute authority. This paradigm was based on the notion that the individual under investigation was considered an object of proof, subject to the application of torments, whippings, and punishments for the purpose of obtaining a confession. Historically, the confession stood as the ultimate proof, being the undisputed queen of evidence. Fortunately, in the evolution of these powers, this approach has been abandoned, giving the process greater impartiality and protection of individual rights.

It should be emphasized that, in contrast to the judge's discretion in this context, what was known as the principle of standardized evidence was imposed. This principle limited the interpretation and application of the judge's powers, providing a normative framework that guaranteed equity and justice in the development of the inquisitorial process.

This inquisitorial methodology has been relegated for a considerable time. However, many judicial professionals are reluctant to incorporate the necessary changes in the administration of justice. This reluctance is based not only on the habitual nature of their roles but also on a lack of confidence in the ability of litigants to perform their functions effectively. There is a fear of not being able to uncover the truth behind events.

The substantial difference manifests itself when the judge personally assumes the investigation and promotes proceedings based on preconceived opinions, prejudices, or newly acquired information. In this act of assumption, the judge becomes responsible for the decisions he or she makes in accordance with his or her function, as opposed to when he or she depends on third parties to carry out this power. This paradigm shift requires a transformation in consciousness and an extensive training process, as urging judges to abandon the old role of inquisitors demands an adjustment in their approach.

Another fundamental characteristic of the inquisitorial regime is also highlighted: the closed doors and little control of the parties. The monopolization of functions by the judge did not favor the active participation of the prosecutor or the parties in the discussion of a matter under analysis. Moreover, this method was characterized by being predominantly written, which limited the judge's knowledge of those involved unless they were about to receive a sanction.

In this context, it is vital to remember that the inquisitorial system, with little control over the parties, as well as written and secret proceedings, distanced justice from public perception and generated distrust in society. The transition to the mixed method in many Latin American countries, including Argentina, has introduced a written phase and an oral hearing but has posed challenges, such as the incorporation of written evidence in the oral trial.

The convergence of written and oral methods in the mixed process has generated problems, allowing the introduction of evidence by reading in the oral trial, which has affected fundamental principles such as contradiction, immediacy, and the right of defense at trial, leading to erroneous sentences. Although the inquisitorial process represented an advance at the time, its limitations, such as the tendency of the judge to retain investigative powers, highlight the need for more equitable systems.

Yet, despite having been largely banished, it persists in several countries, especially those under authoritarian regimes where democracy does not prevail, as is the case in China and some Middle Eastern countries. The prevalence of this system is also manifested in the culture of societies that demand, often through public denunciations, that the mere accusation automatically translates into a condemnation, a phenomenon encouraged by the media – and today's social networks – which do not always disseminate the crucial principles that should be promoted.

On the other hand, the accusatory system regulates the ways in which the hearing process must be carried out.

It is based on a series of fundamental guarantees, establishing limits for its operators. In a way, it is a projection of the individual and procedural guarantees established in the national Constitutions of our countries. The affected individual is in a position to claim, almost on an equal footing, before an impartial judge or jury so that the person who committed the harmful action or omission receives his punishment or makes reparation in some way and in accordance with the law.

Even that individual may be accused of committing terrible deeds; however, in the exercise of criminal prosecution, not everything is valid since there are certain areas on which it cannot be advanced, nor can it be exercised in any way.

For this reason, there is data that is truly revealing. Those countries whose governments are authoritarian or similar have inquisitorial procedural systems. Those countries where the exercise of power is democratic or liberal have accusatory procedural systems. And those that are undergoing a transition or are not very well defined have mixed processes.

The problem experienced in these countries with mixed processes is mainly that the rules are not clear, and citizens live in a deep disillusionment with justice since the law is not applied evenly for all. Therefore, this legal insecurity generates many conflicts that are resolved outside the legal system. That is why I insist that training in oral litigation can be the key to consolidating the necessary bases of understanding and making the qualitative leap that will allow the overthrow of that oppressive system and move to one of full validity of guarantees and principles.

The improvement of this procedural method is manifested both in its view of the individual as a subject of law and in the creation of new roles in the pursuit of justice.

Orality, an essential characteristic of the adversarial process, divides the procedure into stages that, conducted through oral hearings, demand a profound knowledge of the roles and functions to be performed by litigants and operators both inside and outside the judicial sphere.

Therefore, the transparency inherent in the adversarial process – by publicly displaying both our competencies and the possible shortcomings in the preparation of lawyers and judges – is essential to restore the legitimacy of the justice system.

It is, therefore, pertinent to reflect on the importance of acquiring knowledge and skills to resolve controversies and disputes through an informed and updated approach.

In this sense, the adversarial process is presented as the most evolved method of adjudication today, providing a robust and equitable framework for the administration of justice.

However, it is imperative to reflect on the historical context of the inquisitorial process to know its characteristics since its features, ways of being exercised, and vices may be present in our judicial systems, and it is necessary to warn about it in time. Then, we will discuss what is involved in the implementation, operation, and performance within the adversarial system.

Since the principle of the presumption of innocence is fundamental in the field of justice, which is the instance where legal disputes must be resolved, it is important to note that the inquisitorial system has not been completely eradicated from all countries and cultures. Hence, it is crucial to highlight certain considerations as observers and agents of the justice system in order to preserve and guarantee respect for individual guarantees in each case in which we intervene.

- ➢ First, as legal professionals, we have the responsibility to ensure the proper application of legal principles in each particular case. In this sense, it is necessary to focus on safeguarding the rights enshrined in the Constitution, communicating to society the importance of respecting these legal foundations. Lawyers play an essential role as communicators and educators, transmitting to society the validity of inalienable principles that must be preserved in any judicial process.
- ➢ Secondly, our work as lawyers involves being agents of peace, acting as representatives of the various demands of society and the parties involved. We contribute to the efficient functioning of justice systems, being essential for the peaceful resolution of conflicts. By demanding optimal performance of judicial systems, we promote social harmony and reduce society's grievances.

That said, the adversarial system - evidently and necessarily - emerges as a significant evolution, overcoming the difficulties inherent in the previous systems and offering a surprisingly effective solution to overcome the challenges present in the preceding methods.

What does the adversarial system of justice mean?

Oral Litigation Maxim 5: "Accustomed to being cheated, we were forced to distrust. So...be wary."

- DH.

Why is it important to know the individual guarantees? Well, because there is always an excuse to advance on them.

Thus, in light of this affirmation, the adversarial accusatory system arises in democratic countries, as it comes to compensate justice for the terrible consequences and violations that, for a long time, the inquisitorial system and the mixed system, respectively, have been dragging along.

Roles in the adversarial accusatory process

1. **Public prosecution:**

The adversarial and accusatory systems, although often used interchangeably, have fundamental distinctions that shed light on the structure of roles and functions. In this context, the Public Prosecutor's office emerges as the entity in charge of bringing charges against a specific individual for the alleged commission of acts classified as crimes by the legislation in force. It is imperative to emphasize that this criminalization has been pre-established by law, this being an essential component of due process of law, an aspect that will be further explored in subsequent discussions.

In the exercise of its function, the Public Prosecutor's Office has the autonomy to present the accusation independently, in compliance with its inherent obligation.

I am opening a small parenthesis to reflect a problem that is currently staining the accusatory process:

It is important to note how some prosecutors play their role in the process.

This authority and certain autonomy in the exercise of public criminal action lead many prosecutors to behave as adversaries of the defense attorney and to sustain accusations without sufficient grounds or to hide information that could favor the accused party in the process.

Or also those who do not know how to distinguish the real from the ideological and join a worrying wave of requesting preventive prisons without proving procedural risks or, even worse, requesting the conviction of people for whom they have not demonstrated guilt.

It is truly alarming that, despite the fact that prosecutors have an obligation to safeguard individual guarantees, including due process and the presumption of innocence, they act as a kind of "anything goes" and commit acts contrary to their duties.

Not to mention the litigation that many litigants engage in unfairly, introducing evidence at the last minute or even in the middle of a trial, forcing the judge to admit it. They are often those who, in spite of the lack of evidence with which they go to trial, sustain accusations and ask for severe sentences because they openly proclaim that the word of the complainant, whom they call the victim, is equivalent to a conviction. And they forget the duty of objectivity that they should imprint on all their actions. Corporal tortures are not exercised in a direct way, as the inquisitorial judges ordered to apply on the body of the accused. However, many times they ask for precautionary measures without reason or support for the escraches and media condemnations. Flagellations that are committed in the XXI Century.

These are issues that really should be open to debate, and I wanted to introduce them in a preliminary way to make it clear that the fact of changing from an inquisitorial or mixed process to an accusatorial one does not solve all the problems. I am convinced that if we do not correct the mentality of the operators (judges and prosecutors are representatives of the state), we will not solve anything in a deep and definitive way.

2. Private prosecution:

Now, returning to the issue at hand, it is important to emphasize that this accusation may be accompanied by a complaint, that is, when the victim joins the process as a plaintiff. However, it is crucial to recognize that the prosecution and the complaint do not always coincide in their perspective, either with respect to the sequence of events or the specific accusation made against the accused. On numerous occasions, the prosecution and the complaint disagree, either in relation to the legal qualification of the crime or even in considering that the offense was perpetrated by another individual. This divergence may be reflected in their submissions to the court, with the prosecution arguing for conviction while the plaintiff may lean towards acquittal. Although rare cases, these discrepancies are a palpable reality, particularly from my personal experience as a prosecuting attorney representing victims.

In criminal proceedings, the prosecution is primarily the responsibility of the Public Prosecutor's Office, which may choose to proceed with the criminal action and bring the accused to trial or, in certain cases, to withdraw the prosecution. The prosecution has the responsibility to present evidence to prove that the accused has committed a crime. It must also follow legal procedures and respect the rights of the accused during the process. It is also responsible for requesting the imposition of a penalty in the event that the defendant is convicted.

In Latin American countries, the plaintiff can assume this power exclusively, dispensing with the participation of the prosecutor, a situation that I have experienced on multiple occasions, achieving convictions without the support of the prosecution.

In addition to the prosecution, which is inherent to the criminal process, there is the defense, which plays an active role. Both parties investigate, develop their theories of the case, and present arguments during the trial. This process involves – in addition to the use of words – the investigation, the development of arguments, the examination and cross-examination of witnesses and experts, as well as the presentation of material evidence.

3. Defense:

The role of the defense is to represent the defendant in a trial. Its primary function is to ensure that the defendant's rights are respected and to present a defense on his or her behalf. The defense attorney must ensure that the process is fair and that evidence is presented to support the defendant's innocence. It is important to note that it is not the defense attorney's responsibility to prove the defendant's innocence but rather to ensure that the defendant's rights are respected and that an adequate defense is presented.

In contrast, the judge, within the framework of an adversarial system, adopts a passive role. This distinctive characteristic significantly differentiates it from its role in mixed or inquisitorial systems. The judge's passivity lies in the impossibility of conducting investigations, proposing evidence, or examining witnesses during the trial oral proceedings, except in exceptional situations. Such limitation seeks to preserve the judge's impartiality until the moment he issues a judgment that puts an end to the litigation.

Likewise, the judge is prohibited from arrogating to himself powers related to the prosecution of the criminal action. Although the judge may consider that the prosecutor is acting improperly, the judge may not assume the role of prosecutor to prosecute the criminal action. Therefore, those who practice law independently should consider the possibility of becoming a plaintiff since the role of the victim, although important, is not sufficient to actively play the role of prosecutor at the conclusion of the trial. This clear demarcation of functions and roles is essential in the criminal process.

Thus, the adversarial accusatory process establishes a clear framework of action for the parties involved: the prosecutor, the plaintiff, and the defense. It also delineates the position of the judge, making it possible to understand the powers and limitations of each actor in the pursuit of the ultimate goal, which is the revelation of the truth.

Orality in the civil process: An inexorable advance

The trend towards orality in the area of civil procedure is not regressing; on the contrary, it is inexorably projecting itself towards continuous progress. Modern procedural codes must incorporate procedures that stand out for their efficiency, in stark contrast to anachronistic regulations. Oral hearings, presided over by judges committed to the search for procedural truth, bring greater visibility to legal acts, speed to procedures, and clarity of expression.

By virtue of this, the imperative of procedural collaboration and the prohibition of misrepresentation of the facts benefit not only the more astute party but mainly the party that has the truth on its side. The combination of these principles not only strengthens the integrity of the judicial system but also contributes to the fairness and transparency that should characterize any legal process.

In contrast to the old written process, where judges, influenced by social pressures, assumed an inquisitorial role, the current system entrusts the responsibility of seeking the truth to the parties in accordance with procedural rules. The judge, while maintaining impartiality, could not conduct independent investigations or suspend hearings to obtain more information.

Here, it is important to emphasize the duty of litigants to know the procedural rules thoroughly, to research their cases meticulously, and to master oral litigation techniques. For a well-researched case is ineffective if it is not properly presented at trial.

In the accusatory process and in the civil process that is developed through oral hearings, the essence is found in the facts, unlike previous systems that prioritized the law. The discussion is centered on the veracity of the facts, the participation of the parties, etc.

The orality and de-formalization of the system seek to get closer to the people and seek the truth without excessive technicalities.

Therefore, every litigator must bear in mind the importance of investigating and presenting the facts in a clear and understandable manner. The objective is to answer the questions that arise when learning about a criminal act. In addition, a free debate between the parties is encouraged to seek information legally and to present their theories strategically.

Unlike the written procedure, in which litigants often built or adjusted their case according to daily events, both the adversarial process in the criminal sphere as well as the orality of the civil process provide the possibility of implementing a work plan. This approach, as can be appreciated, is considerably more orderly and more aligned with people's expectations, being more understandable, accessible, and, above all, friendly to the justiciable, those individuals who are directly involved in the dispute and seek a solution. Today, the aspiration is for dispute resolution methods that are simple rather than complex.

Procedural principles underlying the adversarial process.

These principles, intended to regulate the punitive power of the State in the prosecution of crimes, represent a clear limit to the power of the State over individual guarantees.

At the same time, they constitute a normative framework that determines when and under what conditions the State may advance in the prosecution of crimes, and in the event of a violation of these constitutional guarantees, a sanction is established both for the procedural act in question and for the officials involved.

Second, they act as a framework for both judges and litigants.

As for judges, when they receive procedural acts that violate individual guarantees, they must exercise their role of direction and control.

Likewise, they provide a method of control over the actions of other intervening parties or agents, making it possible to question and annul procedural acts that violate these guarantees, such as illegal searches, arrests without warrants, or confiscations that violate the right to property.

For litigants, they provide guidance on how to act, reminding them that they are the ones who must comply with these principles in the first place. For example, a prosecutor cannot justify an illegal search, even in the context of a complex investigation.

The latter must refrain from using results obtained by violating constitutional guarantees, thus reaffirming the commitment to a justice system that prioritizes respect for fundamental rights.

Principles of the adversarial accusatory system

Compliance with constitutional and procedural rules and guiding principles is essential to ensure the integrity and fairness of the justice system.

1. Orality

One of the fundamental foundations of the current legal system lies in the principle of orality. It should be noted that, unlike the inquisitorial procedures - which were characterized by their eminently written nature - and the mixed process, which underwent a significant evolution by being deployed in two phases: one written and the other oral. Within the framework of the adversarial process, an entirely oral judicial paradigm was consolidated, in which the various disputes were resolved through oral hearings. This model is not limited only to the trial and the oral and public debate but also includes other resolutions, such as requests for preventive detention by the prosecutor, requests for release by the defense, and requests for seizure by the plaintiff, among other precautionary measures. In addition, it extends to addressing litigation through alternative dispute resolution methods, all under the approach of oral hearings.

Orality, as a guiding principle, entails the observance of other principles that will be addressed in due course. However, it is worth noting that one of the most notable benefits of this approach lies in the direct access to the judicial offices. In contrast to the old practice of resolving disputes on an individual basis, judges are now open to direct interaction with the parties involved. This change is fundamental because, in the past, judges decided on important issues in people's lives without meeting face-to-face with them, which led to misunderstandings and prejudices.

Therefore, the need for the judge to personally perceive the events of a proceeding, to know the parties, and to appreciate both their verbal arguments and their bodily expressions becomes imperative.

Thus, in addition to making the judge the main witness of the events in the trial, orality also seeks to ensure that he forms his initial impressions, sustains or modifies them as the process progresses, and, finally, that his conviction at the time of issuing a decision is solid and well-founded.

In contrast to previous procedures, where the judge – in isolation – based his decisions on legal manuals, consultations with advisors, or private meetings with his clerk to address complex cases; orality favors the opening of the doors of the judicial office. This makes it possible for the parties to meet the judge, to see him personally, to recognize his humanity, and to allow the judge to understand and even propose alternative solutions in some cases.

The authority emanating from an oral opinion differs significantly from that imposed through a written document since it incorporates elements of direct contact, facial expression, and other dimensions that enrich the decision-making perspective and contribute to the legitimacy of the process. In short, orality not only transforms the nature of the judicial process but also revitalizes the relationship between the judge and the parties, fostering an administration of justice that is more transparent, participatory, and closer to the demands of society.

2. Advertising

The second principle is that of publicity, which encompasses a series of significant considerations for society. To begin with, it is important to remember that acts of government must always be public; that is, they must be subject to citizen scrutiny. This imperative is particularly essential in democratic and liberal countries, where those invested with roles of authority, regardless of their position, are obliged to account for their actions.

In this context, for many decades, the Judiciary has, to a certain extent, escaped this citizen control; however, at present, this scrutiny is materialized through its participation in public oral hearings.

Opening hearings to the public allows for the participation of the parties involved and enables the intervention of interested third parties, members of the general public, and even representatives of the media. By opening the doors of the courts of justice, the active participation of citizens in monitoring the performance of judicial functions is encouraged. In this way, the transparency achieved by publicizing acts of government, especially in the judicial sphere, reinforces the need for this branch of government to be accountable for its decisions.

The presence of the judge in the same courtroom where the trial takes place – together with the parties and their litigants – and under the observation of the public and the press constitutes the impartiality of the process. At the same time, it commits the judge to decide in accordance with the facts presented. This public exposure facilitates the formation of logical and reasonable conclusions by society, which, in turn, acts as a counterweight that prevents unjust resolutions.

The benefits derived from the publicity of judicial acts are substantial. However, this transparency also imposes greater responsibility on both litigants and judges. The work of the lawyers must be carried out with diligence and exhaustive knowledge of the facts of the case since any deficiency will be evidenced before the public hearing. On the other hand, the performance of judges is exposed to the public's evaluation, ensuring that their decisions are reasoned and in accordance with justice.

Thus, publicity not only serves as a means of control over judicial activity but also plays an educational role in society. The openness of the courts to citizen participation contributes to the understanding of individual guarantees and encourages the abandonment of prejudices, thus promoting a more informed appreciation of judicial decisions.

Similarly, the press plays a fundamental role in disseminating quality information, bringing society closer to judicial cases of public interest. Thus, publicity confirms or refutes media convictions, even educates society, and acts as a channel of communication between the judiciary and public opinion.

3. Immediacy

The principle of immediacy imposes on the judge the obligation to have direct contact with all the evidence presented during the trial while prohibiting the delegation of this responsibility to other officials, thus ensuring that the judge is present at each oral hearing and personally perceives the evidence presented.

Immediacy is important because it allows the judge to evaluate the evidence in real time and to ask direct questions to the parties to obtain a better understanding of the facts. In this way, the judge can assess the credibility and probative force of the evidence presented, which contributes to a fairer and more accurate judicial decision.

Similarly, the judge can evaluate the behavior of the parties and ensure that the procedural rights of all parties are respected; he or she can detect possible irregularities and abuses that could affect the fairness of the process and correct them in a timely manner.

Immediacy strengthens the legitimacy of judicial decisions by ensuring that they are based on truthful information gathered during the trial, without the possibility of resorting to the reading of files or documents outside the hearing. This principle is essential to preserve the impartiality and integrity of the judicial process.

4. Concentration

Principle number four, known as the principle of concentration, establishes the imperative need to carry out -preferably in a single hearing or in simultaneous hearings- as many procedural acts as possible. However, such concentration must be executed with prudence, avoiding fatigue among the participants as a result of the duration of these procedural acts. It is well known that participation in oral hearings imposes a significant burden on both the litigants and the judges, so an excessive extension of the acts must be avoided, preserving the quality of attention and avoiding the decrease in efficiency over time.

This principle, in addition to advocating multiple procedural acts in the same hearing, as mentioned above, also aims to allow the judge to retain relevant information about the events. The quality of this information is crucial, considering that the passage of time can affect the memory of all persons involved. Imagine the scenario in which a judge receives opening arguments and opening statements on a simple homicide case on one day and, the next day, faces arguments on an aggravated homicide or testimony from another case. In such circumstances, there is a risk of confusion as to the outcome, the intentions of the litigants, or even the interpretation of the evidence presented. This situation, as is evident, carries significant dangers for the administration of justice.

In addition to promoting the concentration of procedural acts in a single hearing, this principle emphasizes the importance of conducting them without excessive interruptions. Although consolidation in a single day may not be feasible due to the number of acts or the complexity of the case, it is urged that, in the event of multiple sessions, these should be carried out without prolonged time gaps that could compromise the integrity of the information. The loss or confusion of data due to deterioration caused by the passage of time is a risk that must be prevented, especially considering the limited capacity of human memory.

The principle of concentration, in addition to expediting the process, also seeks to preserve the coherence and quality of the relevant information without undermining other fundamental principles of the legal system. Speed, in this context, should not translate into a detriment of the other principles governing due process of law.

5. Contradiction

This principle stands out as one of the most valuable and characteristic elements in the adversarial process. Contradiction, in this context, gives the litigants the right to confront all the facts, examine all the evidence presented, and discuss the application of the law proposed by their adversary. This manifestation of contradiction is clearly evidenced during the direct examination of a witness by the Public Prosecutor's Office, followed immediately by cross-examination by the defense. This process makes it possible to refine the information presented, emphasizing that in this trial, the parties act as adversaries immersed in a competitive logic.

That said, the competitive logic of this method of litigation is based on confrontation, where each side strives to identify the weaknesses of its opponent. Litigants operate under a pugilistic dynamic, in which they seek to attack and defend in order to demonstrate the validity of their thesis and discredit the opponent's theory of the case. This competitive approach drives a constant two-version contest, where each litigant seeks to prevail by persuading the judge of the correctness of his or her position.

The uniqueness of this approach is revealed when considering the hypothetical scenario of a star witness' testimony. Although it might initially be presented as an absolute truth, cross-examination by the opposing party reveals possible weaknesses, inconsistencies, or underlying interests in the statement. This cross-examination process, inherent to the adversarial system, plays a crucial role in identifying flaws in the evidence presented and, therefore, contributes to obtaining quality information for the judge.

Likewise, the adversarial process facilitates contradiction, in contrast to the limited ability to directly contradict the judge's interrogations. This principle allows litigants to refine the information presented, preventing the acceptance of biased or inaccurate versions. In the absence of contradiction, the risk of the judge forming an erroneous opinion increases considerably. Therefore, it is essential to emphasize that contradiction does not seek to restrict the judge's activity but rather falls on the responsibility of the litigants, who play a fundamental role in the presentation and questioning of evidence.

In sum, contradiction stands as a fundamental pillar in the adversarial process, allowing the exhaustive review of the information presented at trial. This principle serves the search for truth and highlights the importance of the judge's role in the resolution of disputes and the control of emotions that may arise during the exercise of contradiction in live hearings.

6. Principle of equality of parties

As one of its essential pillars, the principle of equality of the parties is vital to the adversarial process. Fairness between the parties, both prosecuting and defending, is essential to the integrity of the judicial process. This principle recognizes that equality cannot be achieved solely through the presence of an impartial judge but also by ensuring that litigants, regardless of their professional status, have equal access to procedural resources and opportunities.

Equality of parties implies that, despite the differences in the nature of their roles, the acting parties must be treated impartially by the judge. The latter has the responsibility to ensure that the procedural arms are equitably distributed, avoiding favoring one party over the other.

The judge may not grant unjustified preferences, disproportionate time, or undue advantages to any of the parties during the course of the trial. Equality of parties imposes the obligation to grant litigants equal time for both the investigation of the case and their representation at trial.

Preserving the equality of the parties is not only about the time allowed but also about the impartial handling of disputes and the resolution of possible imbalances that may arise. It is essential that the judge act as a zealous guardian of the principle of fair play, avoiding procedural trickery and ensuring that both litigants have equal opportunities to express their arguments and present evidence.

At times, there has been a tendency to undermine these principles by claiming that certain roles have more weight or hierarchy in society. It is imperative to reject this notion and ensure that all participants in the process have equal opportunity and treatment, whether the victim, the accused, the litigant in the lawsuit, or the representative of the prosecution or the defense.

And it is the judge, as the guardian of the equality of the parties, who must ensure compliance with the rules of the game and procedural norms to guarantee that the litigants participate fairly and have the same procedural opportunity to present and prove their arguments at trial.

Adversarial vs. Inquisitorial System (See Chart on the next page)

Adversarial	***Inquisitorial Process***
It is based on the presumption of innocence of the accused.	*The defendant is considered guilty until proven innocent.*
The process focuses on the end result: objective truth and justice.	*The process focuses on procedure and the judge's authority.*
The prosecutor is responsible for presenting evidence and convincing the jury or judge of the defendant's guilt.	*The judge has the responsibility to investigate, interview witnesses, and collect evidence.*
The accused has the right to defense counsel and the right to confront his accusers.	*The accused does not have the right to defense counsel and cannot confront his accusers.*
The evidence is presented before an impartial judge, and the defendant has the opportunity to rebut it.	*The judge is the one who collects the evidence and makes the final decision without giving the defendant an opportunity to refute the evidence.*
The investigation is conducted prior to trial, and evidence is presented at trial.	*Investigation and trial occur at the same time.*
The trial is public, and citizens have the right to attend and observe.	*The trial is private, and only the parties involved may attend.*
The jury or judge makes the final decision based on the evidence presented.	*The judge has the final decision regardless of the evidence presented.*
The process is divided into clear and distinct stages.	*The process is not divided into distinct stages and may be less predictable.*
The evidence must be presented to the court in the form of admissible evidence.	*Evidence may be presented to the judge in any form and may be accepted even if it is not admissible.*
The defendant is not required to testify at his own trial.	*The defendant may be compelled to testify at his own trial.*
Faster procedures due to the need to meet deadlines and legal requirements.	*Proceedings may be slower due to the need to collect evidence and the judge's authority in the process.*
The prosecutor and the defense have a more active role in the process.	*The judge has a more active role in the process.*
The parties have the right to appeal an unfavorable decision to a higher court.	*The parties do not have the right to appeal an unfavorable decision.*
The burden of proof is on the prosecutor to prove guilt beyond a reasonable doubt.	*The burden of proof is on the accused to prove his innocence.*

What makes the adversarial process advantageous?

Have you ever wondered what the community expects from the justice service?

- ➔ The protection of individual rights and the presumption of innocence: everyone is considered innocent until proven guilty in a fair and equitable trial.
- ➔ Its function is to safeguard citizens from potential abuse by the State.
- ➔ Works to control bias in the courtroom environment.
- ➔ Burden of proof: the burden of proof is on the prosecuting party to prove beyond a reasonable doubt that the accused is guilty.
- ➔ Right to a fair and public trial: the accused has the right to a fair and public trial, with all the necessary procedural guarantees.
- ➔ Right to defense: the accused has the right to be represented by a defense attorney and to present evidence in his defense.
- ➔ Right to confront witnesses: the accused has the right to confront and question the witnesses presented by the prosecuting party.

The world of justice is constantly evolving and adapting to respond to the needs of an increasingly demanding society. In this sense, the adversarial process represents an innovative alternative that seeks to bring justice closer to what really matters: the needs of people and their welfare.

In addition, this system promises answers in a timely manner while focusing on transparency and the accompaniment of the victim throughout the process. In other words, it seeks to achieve a more efficient, accessible, and humane justice system that truly responds to the demands of a society that demands concrete and effective solutions.

PROFESSIONAL ADVICE

Remember that you play a fundamental role in society and that it is up to you, to a large extent, to make the adversarial system work and prosper.

THE WINNING STRATEGY: A STRONG THEORY OF THE CASE

"To be successful, you have to develop the courage to think as others are afraid to think."

Did you know that? When the oral trial arrives, the die is already cast, and whether it is good or bad will depend on your preparation. So, if you want your case to succeed, your clients to appreciate you, your adversaries to admire you, and the judges to respect you, you need to know how to prepare yourself. What does this preparation, both personal and in your role as a litigator, prosecutor, or even judge, consist of? Let's explore all the options together.

But first, you have to know that talking about case theory is talking about one of the most important concepts in the legal field; it is a crucial tool to bring any case towards a successful outcome. But what exactly does case theory refer to?

I'll illustrate it with an example...

Can you imagine waking up every day not knowing what you are going to do, drifting? Can you imagine this happening every day of your life? I'm sure you'll say no, that's impossible. However, this is how many colleagues and judges also take their lives and their cases!

Simply put, a theory of the case is the strategy a lawyer uses to present his or her case to a judge or jury. In its broadest sense, it refers to the coherent story that the lawyer constructs, based on adequate prior research, to explain the facts and present his arguments, which support his position in a given case.

Since the oral trial is a contest that must be resolved within the legal canons and where the most credible and acceptable narrative must win, it is vital that it be logical, coherent, and persuasive, with the sole objective of convincing the judge or jury that the lawyer's position is the correct one.

To us, as operators of the law, the theory of the case provides us with a methodology with which we can work tactically and in advance to achieve a goal. This is nothing more than prior organizational work, which we will be willing to do if we want to find the most useful and effective way to present our case and, therefore, have a better chance of success.

> *The theory of the case serves for all previous stages and later, even for a negotiation.*

Characteristics of the theory of the case

A clear, concise, and easily understood theory of the case is essential to effective strategy. At the same time, this theory must be flexible enough to allow the lawyer to adapt his or her strategy as new evidence emerges or contradictory arguments are presented without altering its overall objective.

Importantly, it also needs to be consistent at all stages of the process. Once presented in the courtroom, the litigant is committed to it to the end and cannot change the version of the facts at later stages. Consistency at all times is critical to the validity and credibility of the theory of the case.

In addition, the theory of the case must be consistent with the actions and statements of the lawyer, the client, and others involved, both inside and outside the process. In this way, the theory of the case becomes the foundation of the lawyer's position and the driving element of the process towards its final resolution, which is the judgment and the resolution of the conflict.

How to develop strategic thinking?

Litigation is a complex and demanding action; it can be a difficult task to face, or it can become an art, a daring maneuver. This will depend on whether and how we assume our role as leading lawyers in each of our cases.

Knowing that the theory of the case requires a methodical and organized procedure and that the oral system in the spaces of legal confrontation does not give room for improvisation, it is necessary that litigators develop the skills that allow them to captain their own cases and direct them to the result they have set for themselves.

Therefore, the four most important skills that every lawyer should cultivate to enrich his or her arsenal as a participant and maker of the adversarial process are the following: leadership, strategy, investigative spirit, and storytelling.

❖ **Leading Lawyer**

The crucial skill of leadership in the lawyer's role is an essential pillar of the lawyer's success. My proposal for a comprehensive work plan focuses on three key aspects: the attorney-client relationship, team leadership, and representation in court.

The lead attorney establishes a connection based on trust and collaboration with the client, recognizing his or her active role in the defense strategy. The authenticity of the case theory is nurtured by the client's life story, ensuring their approval and reflecting their narrative in the litigant's presentation and attire.

Likewise, leadership extends to the team, inspiring a genuine interest in rights and life stories. Diversity of skills is harnessed through brainstorming and collaboration, while team commitment is ensured by inspiring them in shared values. Strategic tasks are assigned to enrich the case.

When it comes to the courtroom, the lead attorney projects an image of integrity and credibility as the most valuable cover letter. The culmination of the theory of the case is reflected in a carefully crafted closing argument, bringing together all the elements of the strategy to masterfully lead in front of the judge.

This work plan positions the lawyer as a leader of integrity and commitment, raising the standards of the profession.

❖ Lawyer Strategist

One of the essential skills that a legal strategist must develop is the ability to map out a methodical and analytical plan to achieve a specific objective. It is crucial to keep in mind both the starting point and the ultimate goal. Case theory is used to avoid improvisation and work with a defined plan, which is essential to the oral litigation process. Case theory is considered to be a guide for the litigator to follow in order to overcome any obstacles that arise. Although it is impossible to foresee every situation that may arise during an oral trial, not having a sound method can lead to worse circumstances that could jeopardize the client's interests and the success of the case.

It is essential to select a solid and inflexible theory of the case and treat it as if it were a marriage. This ensures that the plan is coherent and allows you to deal effectively with any unforeseen events.

❖ Investigating attorney

The lawyer is no longer one who simply waits for information to come to him from the comfort of his office. Instead, he acts as an active investigator, diligently pursuing the relevant facts and evidence necessary to build a strong case for his client.

After visiting the scene and gathering relevant information, the attorney may come to a different conclusion than he could by simply reviewing the file or talking to his client. In addition, he or she will be able to determine what type of evidence will be necessary to prove the facts he or she has identified during the oral trial.

In this regard, it is possible, and I do recommend, that you consult with experts in different areas to identify the points of expertise needed or the professionals that should be subpoenaed. Thus, this information is also useful in determining the law applicable to the case in question and discussing the legal characterization of specific conduct with opposing counsel.

Since he understands himself as the leader and driver of his case, the investigating lawyer seeks knowledge to understand the facts and relationships in order to discover the truth or find elements that allow him to get closer to it when defending his position according to his legal theory.

THE INVESTIGATION → GET TO THE FACTS

A good investigation requires us to visit the place where the events occurred in order to gather valuable information that our clients are unable to provide and that is not found in the testimonial or performance records. This detailed information will be crucial at trial and will allow us to present ourselves as the person with the most knowledge about the case.

Information gathering may include taking photographs, recordings, sketches, and interviews with witnesses who have not been previously consulted. In addition, it is important to investigate our client and learn about his reputation in the area where he lives, his professional background, as well as his relationship with his family and friends.

We must also investigate the witnesses that our client provides us with to ensure that there are no surprises during the trial. It is essential to know the conditions of perception of the witnesses, their work schedule, and their relationship with our client or the parties involved in the case. These aspects will help us to identify the strengths and weaknesses of our case and to anticipate possible arguments of the opposing party.

Now, let's start to develop a story...

❖ Storytelling lawyer

After choosing the position to be defended at trial, the litigator must draft a detailed and persuasive version of the facts involving the protagonists and describe the conflict that gave rise to the judicial process. The research conducted by the lawyer will include relevant details about the scene, motives, and events that led to the dispute.

The purpose of this persuasive narrative is to answer the questions that naturally arise and to present the outcome of the case and its significance. The theory of the case, which is developed during the investigation, must be present in the story that the attorney will present verbally.

This skill is fundamental to bringing justice to the public, allowing the person being represented to be known beyond the label imposed by the case at hand. The lawyer's goal is to persuade jurors to accept his or her version of the facts and to identify with the perspective of the defendant.

How to build a theory of the case?

As we have already seen, the theory of the case is the guide, the GPS that leads the action of the litigant from the beginning and throughout the process. However, in order to build a theory of the case, three elements must be taken into account, and when any of them is missing, our thesis or theory becomes ineffective.

Elements that make up the theory of the case

1) Factual propositions → The facts.

In oral proceedings, the issue starts with the question: what really happened? The judge, whose competence is to ensure truth and justice, will at all times be dedicated to providing clarity and seeking answers to this question; that is why you, the litigant, must provide a clear and convincing explanation.

The starting point for an adequate construction of the theory of the case is the preliminary investigation. Considering that in a given matter, the conflict is generated by the presentation of different versions of the same fact, the litigant must try to clarify how the events unfolded and seek to approach the version that is closest to the truth of the evidence.

To carry out this preliminary research, I usually use and recommend in my classes a foolproof system that I show you below:

- **Method 5 "W" + "H".**

Who?	*Who?* ***Who are the protagonists of this story?*** ***Who is the victim?*** ***Who is the victimizer?***
What?	*What?* ***What has happened between them?*** ***What is the event that gives rise to this research?***
When?	*When?* ***When did the event originate - last - end?***
Where?	*Where?* ***Where were the perpetrator and victim located?***
Why?	*Why?* ***Why did the event originate?*** ***What caused it?***
How?	*How?* ***How did this event that I have subject to investigation happen?***

By answering these questions, we will already have the central information of the matter, and it will serve for the successive stages: opening argument, cross-examination, and closing argument.

Likewise, and in my opinion, it is also necessary to carry out a SWOT analysis of the factual propositions; this means to look for the strengths or weaknesses of one's own case and that of the adversary.

- **SWOT Analysis**

STRENGTHS WEAKNESSES OPPORTUNITIES THREATS

By applying this analysis to our case, we will avoid the common mistake of analyzing the facts from a single point of view, which reveals inefficient and incomplete work, and therefore, such practices should be strongly avoided.

Thus, taking into account the adversary's point of view and the different points of view that arise from the facts is the most favorable way to have a more general, objective, and comprehensive view of the matter.

It should be emphasized that the litigant can adopt the position that best serves the purpose of achieving persuasive and effective communication; that is, after listening to the various interpretations of the witnesses and parties involved and their points of view, he can use the most coherent version that best serves his thesis. In other words, we are not obliged to rigidly follow the client's position.

Moreover, in the task of establishing a comprehensive theory of the case, it is necessary to take into account not only judicial issues but also detrimental issues, such as the life of the assisted person in general.

By this, I mean that our theory of the case must be in line with the client's life, history, profession, personal relationships, business relationships, and background. Let us remember that there must be no hint of contradiction; otherwise, our strategy could collapse like a house of cards.

The phases of the work on factual propositions:

A. *Preliminary investigation* consists, as far as possible, of investigating witnesses, those who act, requesting and reviewing the cameras placed on the public road. Request the opinion of experts. To investigate the opposing party. And other actions deemed necessary.

B. *List the facts in* order to clarify which are the strongest, i.e., those that the opposing party will not be able to refute, and establish which are the weaknesses and threats of the case to make the proper preparation and be able to explain them. Remember, in litigation, your weakness is the adversary's strength.

C. *Analyze the facts* using the method of superimposition of factual propositions; in other words, determine the strength of a factual proposition by comparing it with another equally reasonable and credible factual proposition.

In short, after executing the previous research and having as much information as possible, we must separate the strong facts, know the weaknesses, and discard the conclusions; knowing how to differentiate if the data provided are based on prejudices or if they are supported by an objective view is necessary. Therefore, it is supremely important to do good research and list the facts for the second stage: to look for evidence to prove and support the thesis.

2) Evidentiary elements → Search for evidence to support the factual propositions.

In any adversarial process, there is a prevalence of facts over law. This allows us to demonstrate or prove live that, in the matter in question, the facts happened the way we explained them.

This is why the process of gathering evidence to substantiate factual propositions is of vital importance to the construction of the theory of the case; consequently, the litigator's ability to develop investigative skills becomes a paramount requirement.

Any evidence that the litigant gathers to defend his thesis must meet three requirements:

- → *Legality of obtaining:* the principles of good faith and procedural loyalty dictate the prohibition of obtaining any evidentiary element in contravention of procedural regulations or individual guarantees. In other words, the litigant, who considers himself honest, may not make use of any evidence that has been obtained illegally or make use of improper evidence.
- → *Relevance:* orality implies and is inclined to brevity and economy of language. This property does not escape from legal practice; likewise, the trial or oral hearing requires us to be precise and present in a brief but very clear and coherent manner; the most convenient and useful elements for our case.
- → *Credibility:* the task of persuasion, of convincing that every litigator faces when taking on a case, must be supported at all times by evidence that is in line with the story; this evidence must be consistent and fit the theory of the case that we have built. That is, it needs to be credible and aligned with the image and position we want to convey in order to comply with this principle.

3) The law - Legal theory

Legal theory is the theoretical basis that supports the argumentation and evidence to be presented during the trial. In essence, it refers to the interpretation and application of the laws and rules governing the case in question. In order to develop a solid legal theory, it is necessary to carry out an exhaustive analysis of the legislation and jurisprudence related to the subject matter, as well as to have a deep knowledge of the legal system in which the process is framed.

In this sense, legal theory is a key element for success in any litigation. A well-founded and well-argued legal theory can be the difference between a victory and a defeat in a legal case. In addition, it allows lawyers to anticipate and refute possible arguments of the opposing party, which increases their chances of success.

It is important to emphasize that legal theory is not an isolated element in the theory of the case but is interconnected with other key elements, such as the facts of the case and the evidence to be presented at trial. Therefore, it is critical that attorneys conduct a thorough analysis of each of these elements in order to build a strong and compelling theory of the case.

Simply put, its importance lies in its ability to interpret and apply the laws and rules governing the case at hand in a sound and reasoned manner. Therefore, it is essential that lawyers devote time and effort to developing a sound legal theory to increase their chances of success at trial.

Key factors of the case theory

➢ *Narratives of the facts*

One of the key factors in the theory of the case is the factual narrative. A good narrative needs to be clear, coherent, and convincing. It also needs to set out the full story of what happened and how the client was affected. It is important that the narrative be tailored to the audience and designed to appeal to the feelings and reasons of the jurors.

➢ *Motives*

Motives are the goals or intentions that prompt clients to act in a particular way. The theory of the case must answer the question of what motivated our client to take the action that gave rise to the controversy. Accordingly, we litigators are charged with presenting these reasons in a clear and convincing manner to demonstrate that the client acted justifiably and reasonably.

➢ *Emotions*

Emotions play an important role in the theory of the case. Litigation can be a very emotional process for all parties involved. Capturing and using emotions appropriately to connect with the judge or witnesses is an essential prerequisite to building a much more persuasive theory of the case and swaying them in favor of your position.

To clarify, what are the advantages of working with a case theory?

- It allows us to work ahead of time with a strategy and focus on concrete results.
- It provides us with a methodology to be able to tell our version of what really happened; to delimit the hypothesis we will try to test.
- It is very useful in the preliminary stages (mediation and conciliation), as well as when making written submissions, intervening in a preliminary hearing, and when we must defend our position in an oral trial.
- It gives us coherence, organization, and the benefit of being able to sustain a determined position-thesis during the process.
- It functions as a guide that directs the litigant from the beginning to the resolution of the matter.

The theory of the case has the ultimate goal of telling a story that is credible, simple, and persuasive to the audience in order to assert our truth. This requires a logical, congruent, coherent, and plausible story.

I illustrate it with a brief example.

In order for you to appreciate the importance of building a theory of the case following the elements previously expressed, I ask you what would happen if you were to defend a man accused of sexually abusing, killing, and throwing a teenager into a garbage can.

An abhorrent and heartbreaking event. And the strategy of your case is, almost exclusively, to discuss incriminating evidence based on certain contamination in the DNA samples taken from the victim's body.

And that this genetic profile (which you question) is the one found under the victim's fingernails.

So, following your plan, in your opening statement, you mention the procedures used for the trace collection. During the development of the process, you interrogate experts who explain how the trace collection procedure is, what protocols must be complied with, what establishes the chain of custody, and why there could or could not be contamination.

Then, you insist on the same in your closing argument and overlook the circumstances surrounding the act, the attitude adopted by the accused, and other traces that directly link him.

Do you think your strategy will succeed?

Clearly not. In a case like this, with incriminating evidence, your alibi should include the elements we share with you in this chapter, among which are the fundamental obligation to build a persuasive, credible story and to refute with the same force the story your adversary has built.

If you only rely on a biased scientific theory but also cannot answer in an alternative way, the classic questions that everyone here is asking about what happened, how it happened, when it happened, and where, your theory of the case will fail no matter how hard you try.

PROFESSIONAL ADVICE

- ★ *Do not underestimate any case; all are important.*
- ★ *Maintain open communication with your customers.*
- ★ *Inform of the risks without scaring and the probabilities of success without generating excessive hopes.*
- ★ *Keep your word.*
- ★ *Work on your weaknesses. Build on your strengths.*
- ★ *Research your opponent.*
- ★ *Study the judge and his rulings.*
- ★ *Build a persuasive story (for creditability)*

IMPORTANCE OF THE THEME-SUBJECT AT THE ORAL TRIAL

Don't underestimate the power of an effective slogan!

As I mentioned in the previous chapter, the ability to persuade in an oral trial is critical for any litigator. For this reason, oral litigation techniques make use of the theme-topic concept in order to ensure that the presentation of the case meets that fundamental (and desirable) requirement: a convincing and effective presentation of the case.

In this chapter, I will show you how to identify the theme and slogan of your cases and how to work this tool in detail; to do so, we must first analyze both words separately.

The word "Motto" if we refer to it etymologically; we have to go back to the Latin root *"lemma"* which in turn comes from the Greek "*lêmma"* and its meaning points to the phrase or title that encloses the central idea of a job, group or organization, event, among others. **It is the statement that captures the spirit and the main idea and is used as a guide to convey a specific message.**

In other words, a tagline is the key to achieving the desired understanding and impact on the reader or audience. By expressing an idea or intention, the tagline becomes a powerful tool to inspire, motivate, and connect with the target audience.

On the other hand, the issue has more to do with the background of the matter, with the antecedents that triggered the events; we relate it to the previous emotions or relationships that the parties have or have not had. For example, racial hatred, xenophobia, gender-based violence, greed, etc. Its origin is given by the Latin name *"thema,"* whose origin comes in turn from the Greek term *"θέμα: théma."*

So, in my opinion, these two terms have very different meanings; however, one depends on the other. In order to be able to identify what our slogan will be, we must first have clearly defined the subject of our business.

The slogan will be exercised according to the theme and will convey the soul, the vital substance of our theory seeking to appeal to the emotions and cause a great impact on the judge and the rest of the audience.

The motto is thus a fundamental principle that is intrinsically linked to the theory of the case and to the opening and closing arguments. Although it is sometimes overlooked in relation to these instances, its importance should not be underestimated **because it is even useful to us as a linchpin when examining and cross-examining witnesses and experts.**

By this, I mean that the slogan is and should be that short and precise phrase with which a position is established that will proceed to be argued, and the intention of the closing argument is implied. It is also used outside the jurisdiction of the court, normally, to make known to the public opinion -if it has media characteristics- the vicissitudes of the case that deserve to be disclosed. Since leading lawyers must be prepared to exercise their role both inside and outside the courthouse, synthesizing in a single sentence the values and history that we are representing can make a difference in communication.

A slogan could be: "Judges ordered to reduce the sentence of a serial rapist, considering it cruel and inhuman." This was the slogan I used in the media and in the appellate instances of a very controversial case in Argentina.

The objective of any Motto is to appeal to the emotionality of those in charge of resolving the dispute and of the spectators, conveying in a clear and concise manner the fundamental idea of the case that has broken justice and, equally important, the idyllic of justice that is sought to be achieved.

In short, **the slogan is the key that unlocks the door to a fair resolution of the conflict since it summarizes in a single memorable phrase the whole issue to be debated.** So don't underestimate its power. With the right slogan, you can convey the very essence of your case and move those involved to fight with you in the pursuit of legality.

Expert litigators work this tool conscientiously to ensure that its use is most effective and persuasive at all stages of the judicial process since the proper use of the slogan can make the difference between winning and losing in a trial or oral hearing.

Purpose of the theme

Impact with a memorable phrase to achieve grip.

As we already know, when it comes to an oral trial, one of the most important aspects is to have a clear and effective strategy to persuade the judge to make a decision in our favor. This is where the central theme and theme of our case comes into play.

The slogan is like a gift to the judge, a short and powerful phrase that summarizes the conflict at hand and appeals directly to his or her logic and emotions. That is why it is vital to work hard on the research of our case in order to abstract the central theme and express it clearly and concisely through the slogan.

Thus, during the trial, the motto becomes our best ally, constantly reminding us of the main objective. We should evoke it during opening arguments, repeat it during witness statements and presentation of evidence, and mention it again during closing arguments. This methodology of working with the theory of the case allows us to convey in a simple and clear manner what the matter in question refers to, resulting in a more concise and understandable exposition for the judge.

In short: a powerful slogan is the key to persuading the judge and jury and to be more likely to succeed in our case.

How do I find the theme for my case?

PASO	ESTRATEGIA
1	Explora las emociones detrás de los hechos. Analiza motivaciones: ¿Venganza, odio, codicia?
2	Enfócate en la psicología de los eventos. Comprende las razones y la motivación detrás de las acciones.
3	El alegato de apertura es clave. Presenta el tema eficazmente, responde preguntas clave sobre los motivos.
4	Para hallar el lema, resume la idea central de manera sencilla y memorable.
5	Crea una frase ética y moral que llame al sentido de justicia.
6	Considera la audiencia: jueces técnicos valoran hechos; jurado popular se guía por la empatía.
7	Realiza un brainstorming creativo. Permite todas las ideas, genera enfoques efectivos.
8	Utiliza pruebas materiales y testimoniales para obtener el lema.
9	Identificación: Si la teoría sugiere una identificación incorrecta, demuéstralo.
10	Explora redes sociales, experiencias personales para inspiración.
11	Asegúrate de que el lema sea relevante y coherente con la imagen profesional.

So, with regard to the question of how to discover your theme and then synthesize it through a slogan? To do this, it is necessary to go to the emotions that generated the events; I could also say go to the facts but with a more psychological approach; in order to understand the reasons that triggered everything that happened, we must find the motives... the motivation.

In my experience, the theme is the heart of the case, the essence that must be conveyed to the judge and jury in order for them to fully understand what happened. That is why **I want to emphasize the relevance of discovering the theme of a case before presenting it at trial.**

Emotions are often the main driver behind human actions, so when analyzing the background of a case, it is critical to pay attention to the emotions behind the events. "Did they act out of revenge, hatred, remorse, greed, negligence, betrayal or disaffection?"

What has been said so far implies that in order to find the motto and the theme of a case, the approach must go straight to the emotions that gave way to the events in question; the look must be psychological. By doing this, we can understand the motives that triggered everything that happened and find the motivation behind our client's actions. This will allow us to have a complete understanding of the background and present it with clarity and conviction to the judge and jury.

At trial, the opening argument is the key moment to present the theme of our case effectively. We must respond quickly and effectively to the questions the judge and members of the court are asking, especially those related to why the facts are true. Correctly answering these questions is essential to getting the judge and jury to empathize with our client and render a fair decision in his or her favor.

Finding the motto...

After addressing the issue, you will have to figure out how to express it through the slogan. You should start by asking yourself, "How can I summarize and highlight the central idea of my case theme in a simple and memorable way?"

This sentence is similar to the headline of a newspaper or a journalistic article, so it should rescue ethical and moral values, the sense of justice, and common sense, among others.

When we talked about the theory of the case, we emphasized the need for the litigator to become an exhaustive investigator to know the facts in depth and rescue values, which may well be the life story of their client, in order to align our communication with the empathy of the judge and jury; this is referred to in Aristotelian philosophy as *pathos.*

Therefore, we must develop a slogan that has moral and ethical content, and that appeals to the sense of justice and, consequently, generates an impact on the emotions of the judge and the jury.

Popular jury and technical judge

The role of the people's jury and the technical judge in a trial is fundamental. However, when communicating with them, it is important to keep in mind their different approaches.

This is because the technical judge's decisions should be based on logic and verifiable scientific facts. Therefore, it is necessary that we present concrete evidence and a solid argumentation to persuade this type of judge.

On the other hand, the popular jury is made up of citizens who have not studied law and have no contact with any branch of law. Therefore, their decision could be based on their ability to empathize with the arguments presented. To persuade a popular jury, litigants must appeal to emotions and *pathos.* That is, it is essential to present the facts in a clear and accessible manner while conveying the emotion behind the case.

Brainstorming

Brainstorming is an excellent way to spark creativity and encourage discussion among the legal team, investigators, and other stakeholders. By allowing all ideas to be valid, creative, and effective, slogans and approaches can be generated. So, let your imagination run wild and find the best way to persuade the jury and judge in your next case!

Alternative means of acquiring the slogan

- ➔ It is also possible to obtain the motto by means of material evidence and testimonial statements.
- ➔ Another way to acquire it is through the identification process. For example, if your theory of the case suggests that the identification was incorrect, you can justify it by demonstrating that there was a mistake in the identification, using pictures or attire to illustrate how confusion is possible.
- ➔ We can also refer to statements made on social networks and draw inspiration from our own experiences or popular sayings to find a suitable slogan.

It is important to remember that the tagline must be relevant to the case and cannot be disconnected from it. As lawyers, we must maintain credibility and ensure that the tagline aligns with our professional image. The slogan must be supported by the argument and values expressed in the opening and closing statements, as well as through witness testimony.

Ways to solve the parallelisms of the lemma

When drafting a slogan to represent our legal case, it is critical to keep in mind that our opponent may be doing the same thing. Even a single sentence with a question mark can be interpreted in opposite ways by the disputing parties. Therefore, we need to develop two persuasive stories from two different perspectives, supported by solid evidence to back up our slogan.

Our goal is to convince both the judge and jury, as well as the court in general, that our version of the facts is correct.

To achieve this, we need to be consistent and astute in the presentation of our legal arguments. If our opponent takes our slogan and misrepresents it, we must be prepared to respond with a compelling narrative that disproves it. For success in litigation depends on our ability to persuade the court of our truth.

Let's go to a specific case...

Do you have a slogan to use in the early stages of the process? That's a really great thing. Well, sometimes it happens that we lawyers take on the representation of a case late in the process. This is what happened to me when I took on a case assigned by PROPAQUE (Programa de Patrocinio de Querellas), a mechanism for representing victims of serious crimes who do not have the financial resources necessary to obtain legal representation – jointly run by the Colegio Público de Abogados de la Capital Federal and the Ministry of Justice. I will tell you the most relevant:

At the beginning of 2014, I was summoned from the PROPAQUE office to ask me to assume the representation in a case since I had to replace the previous lawyer. According to Mariana, the secretary, I was not to worry. My role was to present myself as the lawyer of one of the eight victims of a serial rapist. In addition, I was told that the rapist had been sentenced to 50 years in prison and that the defense attorney had filed the corresponding appeal.

My arrival on the case turned out to be a mere formality because "there really wasn't much to do;" nothing could have been further from the truth.

At that time, I met Dr. Ustarroz, who was in the same situation since he assumed the representation of one of the victims due to the resignation of the previous sponsor...

When we came into contact with the file before the Court of Cassation, we discovered that the deadline for submitting our response to the appeal was running and that in order to be able to give it due substantiation, we had to study a file that occupied more than 10 pages, that is to say, 2000 pages. Failure to answer this transfer in due time and form could mean that our clients would have to bear the consequences of a real state of legal defenselessness. At that time, the role of the complaint was subsidiary to that of the Prosecutor.

The prosecutor, who, as we discovered, had supported many of the defense attorney's requests and asked for a reduction of the sentence for the serial rapist.

In addition to this, at that time, my youngest daughter had been hospitalized for pneumonia, which had annulled the capacity of one of her lungs and half of the other. All this was the result of a medical malpractice that had complicated her initial condition.

So, while he cared for her at night in the hospital, he took the opportunity to study the voluminous file.

As I read the heartbreaking testimonies of the victims, my anguish increased, and my fighting spirit grew stronger.

Gradually, I came to understand where the legal conflict lay.

Days later, together with my colleague, we made the pertinent presentations. To my surprise, it was the Prosecutor before that Chamber who requested that the sentence of the serial rapist be reduced because he considered that the declaration of recidivism of the subject implied that he, in fact, could not access parole. Therefore, it should be considered that maintaining the sentence to which he had been sentenced was to grant him cruel, inhuman, and degrading treatment.

Based on the above and citing a number of international norms, he requested a reduction of his prison sentence to less than 30 years when he had already been sentenced to 50. What seemed to be a simple case since it was in the final stages of the process and with a sentence ended up being a case that, due to technical issues, changed the fate of the victims and mine in particular, since it was the first one that opened the doors for me in the media.

That is to say that the Court of Cassation, sharing the arguments of the Prosecutor, had ordered the Trial Court to reduce the sentence of 50 years for the serial rapist. Something totally unusual, which did not meet the rights of the victims to obtain a sentence in accordance with the law.

Alarmed by the news, I began to write notes to the most important newspapers in the country, for which I looked for a striking title that represented and made known the nature of the case.

Thus, the slogan of my case was forcefully stated: **"Judges order to lower the sentence of a serial rapist for considering it cruel and inhuman."**

Imagine the impact generated by journalists and mass media through this powerful slogan. Amazed by the news, they could not believe that such a possibility was being discussed.

The balance of justice was clearly shown. On one side, the 8 women victims of the most savage acts suffered, and on the other side, their rapist, the justice system, having decided to put its fingers and its whole hand on the plate of the condemned man to favor him.

In other words, the focus of attention for these judges was not on the cruel or inhumane nature of the heartbreaking acts of abuse suffered by the victim, which in a short period of time had been committed by this sexual predator, but on the amount of the sentence imposed.

It is important to mention that these judges of cassation had not witnessed the trial, did not know the defendant personally, had not heard the heartbreaking stories of the victims and had not appreciated that the convicted person was a recidivist. They simply limited themselves to ordering the reduction of the sentence imposed despite the fact that it had a legal basis. My position beyond the creation of the slogan is that those two judges of cassation could not force the convicted individual to live in a society with rules when he had clearly demonstrated an absolute detachment from them since he had also been convicted of the same crimes previously.

The case took a thousand turns and was, to the best of my knowledge, the most reviewed case as it went through two different cassation instances.

However, the creation of this Motto opened the door to the media, and I was able to communicate to society how justice works from the inside. I was also able to ensure that the 50-year sentence is maintained, as well as the declaration of recidivism, for which reason it is almost improbable that I will ever be able to leave prison.

This brief but powerful slogan became the marketing for my case; it deeply touched the morale of society and allowed me to give this debate both in court and in the media, exposing the unfairness of the system and also the way in which judges -once again- with their interpretations made the law say what the law does not say, to the detriment of those who had been fighting for justice for years.

The story did not end there. You can find information related to this case at the following links:

https://www.infobae.com/2014/05/28/1568170-lo-condenaron-violador-serial-pero-jueces-quieren-bajarle-la-pena-cruel-e-inhumana/

Consequently, the motto selected in this conflict was the one that allowed us, in the end, to obtain justice even in the final stages of the criminal process.

PROFESSIONAL ADVICE

★ *Not all cases must have a slogan. Many times, we find the theme but not the right words to convey it. Having a theme and conveying it through a slogan* <u>*is a strategic decision by the litigator*</u>*; he is and should be considered responsible for his case from beginning to end.*

★ *Not all slogans and themes fulfill the persuasive function that we want to achieve; this will depend on whether you will present your case in front of a popular jury or a technical judge. The latter bases its decisions mainly on the application of the law, doctrine, and jurisprudence. Therefore, the exposition must be through logos, logic, and scientific verification of the facts.*

★ *The popular jury, on the other hand, like us, applies much more common sense, principles, and maxims of experience and their experiences, which is why you must speak to them through pathos – emotions, motives, explaining why. But appealing to empathy.*

★ *You need to get the motto throughout the trial to respect the ethos and trust of your audience. Therefore, the motto-theme must be in line with the values you need to convey as a litigator to be defended and disseminated by your audience.*

- ★ *It is also essential that your audience understands what the message you are giving is about, that they understand its usefulness, and that they can remember what the case and the story is about.*
- ★ *The last recommendation is that you address it in the opening statement and that you pronounce it loudly but very calmly and confidently (emphasizing important phrases and repeating them) as a fulfillment of a promise in the closing statement.*

UNVEILING THE CLOAK OF TRUTH WITH THE OPENING STATEMENT

A powerful opening statement is like a map that guides the judge and jury to truth and justice.

Many times, lawyers who have the habit of developing strategic thinking and carefully analyzing each step before taking it wonder to what extent it is convenient to show our cards to the adversary. What sense does it make to tell the judge that the events happened in such a way and that Marta, an eyewitness, is going to come and tell him how Pedro took a knife out of the right pocket of his jeans and stabbed Oscar in the back, just because she suspected that he was his wife's lover.

We think that anticipating the move is not good for the case since we are telling our opponent where I am going to hit him and using what. Giving him the opportunity to anticipate the blow and weaken me. Moreover, many times, leaving the door of uncertainty open can give us more security in this strategy of the controversial game that is given in full trial.

If you have thought about this dilemma as I did, I would like to tell you why I have come to the conclusion that we are wrong. To do so, I will use as an example one of the most resonant and emblematic cases in my country, which held the whole community captive.

In the summer of 2020, at the door of a major nightclub, a group of 10 young people was captured by security cameras and cell phones, beating another group and, in particular, several of them attacked with punches and kicking another, who eventually died.

After three years, the oral and public trial of the most resonant and mediatic case of recent times was to take place.

With the images being televised 24 hours a day, 7 days a week, on all channels, such a strong popular opinion was generated that it was assumed that there was nothing to discuss about the facts, the responsibility of each one of the accused, and the penalty to be imposed on them. Everyone was calling for life imprisonment for the 8 defendants who came to the trial.

Another important fact was that the lawyer representing the victim's parents took care of installing a concept about the defendants, calling them "beasts" that "should die in jail."

In every interview given on television channels, radio, and YouTube programs, he repeated the same name, which was installed in the collective conscience of the entire society in Argentina.

On the other hand, the defense attorney had never made any statement until then, maintaining absolute silence. But he had also decided, strategically, to represent the eight defendants without discriminating the intervention that each one could have had in the act and, consequently, to exclude the responsibility of those who had not played any role in the commission of the crime.

But... What was the outcome of that trial?

The month of January began. In Argentina, it is a judicial fair, which means that there is no activity in the courts; no cases can be initiated (except for urgent cases or arrests), and lawyers take advantage of it to take vacations. Well, in January 2023, something unusual happened. Court No. 1 of Dolores -a town of few inhabitants located 200 km from the Federal Capital- had decided that the most mediatic trial in Argentina would start on January 2. All the national and foreign press had stationed their correspondents there. The society was expectant to find out what was going to happen to those 8 young people (between 21 and 23 years old) accused of causing the death of another young man, Fernando Baez Sosa, at the entrance of a very crowded discotheque called "Le Brique," located in the seaside area of Villa Gesell.

Through a YouTube channel, the Supreme Court of Justice of Buenos Aires opened the doors of the courts, and, live, we were all able to witness the beginning of that trial, on which the whole community (laymen and lawyers as well) had already taken a position.

The court gave the floor to the prosecuting parties (public and private) to present their opening arguments. The lawyer representing the victim's parents, a well-known and famous lawyer -very much in the media, by the way- had been in charge of generating all the conditions for the press attention to be 100% there.

The allocution of both prosecuting parties was really simple, somewhat vague, and even somewhat incongruous. But they expressed themselves on the facts, detailing the evidence to be produced and the legal qualification that, according to them, should be applied at the end of the trial. The president of the court gave the floor to the defense attorney, the same one who decided to represent the 8 defendants -everyone, absolutely everyone- both inside and outside the court, was eager to hear it for the first time. After three years of absolute silence, we wanted to know what he had to tell us about it.

The *rating* was rising rapidly, we were waiting for the defender to tell us what happened that night of January 18, 2020. We wanted to know how he would carry out his strategy – the one he kept so secretly, which allowed to involve 8 young people in the commission of a crime that could condemn them to life imprisonment. The crowd clamoring for justice was stationed at the scene. Behind closed doors, the young defendants were there, surrounded by police, in a small courtroom of the small-town courthouse. Speculations were growing by the minute; what would he say about the accused, for example, about those "who did not hit the victim? Or how will he defend the one who kicked him brutally and the other one who filmed part of the event? Or about the other one who harangued? Will he have evidence to offer? Which ones?"

And then the microphone of the defense attorney and his young partner (a lawyer, who was also the sister of one defendant and the cousin of two others) was turned on.

His hesitant words began to be heard but still not understood until he suddenly expressed: "Yes, I have a theory of the case, and that is that my defendants are innocent until proven guilty." And so he closed his presentation.

We were all astonished because, in reality, what he had said meant nothing; it did not allow us to calm the waters nor to understand his position. And even less so to obtain another version of the facts. He did not take advantage of the opportunity to answer all the questions and establish a position that would allow the court to find some clarity regarding the thesis that the defense would face in the trial.

His argument lasted only a few seconds, and he did not express anything about the mechanics of the facts; he did not differentiate the total, partial, or null participation of his clients in the production of the death result. Nor did he question the causal relationship. He did not state the evidence that would support this claim, which, on the other hand, we did not know what it would be. Why was this important? Well, because he did not say anything about the facts, nor about the evidence, much less about the legal theories involved.

There, I felt that the colleague had taken a leap into the void. I wondered if he had a strategy and if the fact of enunciating could benefit or harm him. In the light of the results, as I thought, he was prejudiced by the fact of not expressing himself and wasting the opportunity given by the opening argument. We never knew what the defendants had to say, what their version was, and what charge each of them was facing. The failure to speak out sealed the fate of that trial.

In addition to this case, we analyzed it as an example. Let's analyze together the other reasons why it is necessary -in the adversarial process- to express your position through the opening argument.

Let's see...

What is the point of expressing yourself at the beginning of the trial?

Answer this question with a simple sentence:

"It is the means that oral litigation gives you to conquer your audience from the beginning of the oral and public debate."

The opening argument is like the instruction manual of the case; it tells the judge what the pieces are and their functions, where they should be placed, and how they fit together so that the apparatus will finally start. It is the technique created with the purpose of positively predisposing the court so that it opens its senses to interpret the testimonial and expert statements, as you suggested at the beginning.

What you are looking for is to use the right and appropriate words so that the resolvers will give the evidence the same meaning that you have given it when stating it.

The plea for openness and the conquest of credibility – Maxim of oral litigation

"If you gain confidence with your first presentation, jurors or court members will want you to win that case."

The **leading litigator, who** will be on stage for the first time in this trial, knows that he has to show off, not in the sense of being a Hollywood star, but to prove to everyone present that he knows his case better than anyone else, that he knows all the secrets and that he is there to unveil them.

Meanwhile, the parties – the client, the judge, the jurors, the public, and perhaps, the press – are waiting in the courtroom. They want to hear those brave words; they are anxious to know the other side of the story. And, through the litigator, they want to know who their client is since minutes before they heard the plaintiff say, "This guy was driving under the influence." The litigant takes a glance around the courtroom, observes the judge, and detects in him a little bit of overwhelm; knows that he is tired of listening to long speeches that do not contribute anything useful for his performance and, therefore, it is the litigant who has to generate a minimum of hope, showing a different attitude than the one shown by the rest of his colleagues and opponents.

The **leading litigator** knows all this in advance. We are about to witness the opening speech of a litigator who, in addition to being a leader, is a skilled strategist and investigator, knows very well how to start, what to say first, second, and third; with which phrases he will captivate the audience, what he will say about the evidence, what he will present during the trial and what will be the direction or turn he will take at the end of his presentation. He has even decided beforehand whether he is going to comment on the weaknesses or whether it is better not to anticipate them.

This is so because the function of the opening argument is to enunciate part of the strategy to share it before the Court, although, strictly speaking, it is not necessary to reveal everything you are going to offer or what you intend to obtain by expressing yourself. However, it is necessary to reinforce that it is the means that oral litigation gives you to conquer your audience from the beginning of the oral and public debate.

This tool represents your opportunity to tell the courtroom with confidence that you are there to get justice, to give your side of the story; to promise them that you will prove (with experts, witnesses, and evidence) what really happened. But mostly, it is your chance to show them that you are trustworthy.

The opening statement serves as the table of contents of a book or, perhaps, the movie trailer that will allow you to decide in a fraction of a minute whether it is powerful enough to grab your attention and get you to drop everything you were doing.

A good opening pleading persuasively informs but does not go into details, as suggested by the cover of the book that invites you to open it and read its index carefully, and that after that will determine you to compare it or to continue looking through the shelves of the bookstore. **The lawyer must keep in mind that if he did not conquer at the beginning, he would hardly be able to win that trial at the end.**

The opening argument is the initial presentation made by the parties before the court, whether it is the prosecutor or prosecutor/guilty or defense counsel, plaintiff or defendant. Its purpose is to inform the judge or jury of the facts of the case, what evidence we will use to prove the truth of those facts, and that they really occurred as we have outlined in our presentation; also, we will state the law we seek to apply and finally, our final request: acquittal or conviction, depending on the role we are playing, prosecutor/guilty or defense attorney.

It is important to clarify that these opening arguments are much more than a simple presentation; they are the opportunity and the occasion for the litigants to attract attention and generate empathy in those who will decide the resolutions of the trial.

It is but the cornerstone in the foundation of a strong and solid case, laying the groundwork for the success that will follow.

Functions of the opening statement

Initial and persuasive presentation of the case, to inform the court about the facts and the protagonists.

↓

Establish an expectation and the basis of the argument to be developed during the trial.

↓

Prepare the ground for the presentation testing, which will be carried out a posteriori

↓

To provide the judge (or jury) with the knowledge of the specific case and the tools to resolve it with justice

In the context and development of a trial, in the adversarial system, no phase is as crucial as the opening. This is where you lay the groundwork for the case and the direction the trial will take, trying to shape the perception of the judge and jury. In order to do this, you must earn trust, and this is a difficult task, but not impossible. Why? Below, you will understand what I mean...

Requirements and content of the opening statement to achieve persuasive effect

In keeping with the essence and ultimate goal of the opening statement, the litigant must become the hero of his or her case and, as we have said in past chapters, define a clear objective and work accordingly to achieve it, i.e., develop **leadership skills.**

Since, as a **leader,** he will seek with a clear goal already established in advance that the members of the tribunal will adopt his thesis and fall in love with the case as much as he must.

He must also outline a plan to carry out that objective, which involves a strategy from start to finish, where the litigation **strategist** makes a commitment to himself to follow through and see his plan through to the end.

It is when the debate, the adversarial act, begins that each litigant will present this plan and must tell the judge – like any **investigating** attorney – how much they know about the facts of the case, as well as what evidence they have found and how they will use it to prove the factual propositions.

By virtue of setting forth these facts to make them known to the judge and jurors in a persuasive and convincing manner, the lawyer must also become an expert **storyteller**, thus gaining their adherence to his or her theory of the case.

THE OPENING STATEMENT IS AN ACT OF COMMUNICATION

Oral litigation maxim 6: **"Credibility is the best letter of introduction."**

What is expressed is simple: who would be willing to follow what another person tells them if they don't believe in the words they say?

As we were able to appreciate the real case that we shared as an example in this chapter, we should not underestimate the strength and usefulness of the opening argument for any trial.

In addition to the above, it is important to refer to the fundamental role that the lawyer with a leadership vision must transmit to his audience.

This leadership role in the process will be exercised through his first appearance. It is there where he/she will have to make an impact through his/her speech and body language.

You should demonstrate confidence in yourself and what you say and show the members of the court and jury that because you know so much about the case, you will be the best person to convey all the relevant details to them and, therefore, be the one they should trust when making a decision.

To have such an effect, you must appear to be a trustworthy person.

A leading lawyer can also use a slogan that embodies these universally recognized values within his or her community.

The litigation strategist is aware that every word counts and that is why he selects them carefully in order to achieve understanding by the recipients of his message.

A tedious, boring, confusing, or overwhelming opening speech is useless.

On the other hand, he will insinuate everything he has investigated in order to get others to reach the same confusion.

As a storytelling litigator, you will announce how you will answer those questions, which the judges and/or jurors silently ask themselves and whose answers guide them throughout the trial.

The litigator who seeks to distinguish himself must create and express a discourse that is logical, technical, simple, and emotional at the same time.

So, what conditions must the opening statement meet?

You have to make a good first impression and sustain it.

→ According to Oscar Wilde, "There is no second chance for a first good impression," and this is a truth as big as a temple. Let's imagine that you are in a café and you meet Pablo, a friend from college who comes with Pedro; you greet each other with emotion and affection, and your friend introduces you to Pedro. However, Pedro pays no attention and picks up his cell phone, ignoring your greeting at all times. Then, he finishes talking on the phone and rushes over to apologize to you, but he does so with rude and impolite language.

I suppose that in that very short period of time, you have already formed a bad first impression of Pedro (so have I), and even if Pablo assures you that he is an excellent person and you meet on future occasions, your mind is already predisposed to think of him what his initial behavior conveyed to you.

According to psychology, we are guided during that initial contact by feelings that, in an unconscious way, are generated by people when we have contact for the first time.

It only takes a fraction of a second for us to form an opinion about another person that will unknowingly condition our future relationship.

People analyze another person when they first see them under two metrics.

- *Trust level*
- *Level of self-confidence*

Regarding the level of trust, we seek to discover if the person is sincere about the objectives that he/she transmits to us or that we can deduce, both verbally and gesturally (what he/she does not tell us).

Regarding the level of self-confidence, what we seek to discover is whether that person has a sufficient level of self-belief to meet those objectives that we were able to discover in that first interaction.

Only by answering affirmatively to these two questions that we ask ourselves unconsciously (if he/she is trustworthy and capable) will we be interested in listening to our interlocutor.

Therefore, for us litigators, it is essential to capitalize on this knowledge.

Hence, it is of great importance that our first appearance in the process reflects these virtues that we have just discovered.

Therefore, the litigant must demonstrate to the judge and jury that his objectives are noble and, therefore, he is trustworthy and that he is confident and believes in what he is saying. This is the only way to win over the initiator.

This increases the likelihood that the tribunal members will trust what we say and adopt our position.

But how can we achieve this?

➢ Studying the case in detail.

- ➢ Presenting the case in an orderly fashion and with concrete discourse.
- ➢ Being punctual.
- ➢ Speaking clearly and politely.
- ➢ Being very sure that what we have announced will be fulfilled in the development of the process.
- ➢ Making intelligent use of the body language.

Then, we need to maintain that first good impression with a second good impression:

We aim to sustain what we have built up by strengthening the bonds that we have established with the members of the court throughout the trial, thanks to all our best actions. Therefore, **all our actions must be honorable.**

Information must be accurate and limited.

➔ In order to avoid the undesirable tedium of an overly lengthy presentation or delving into irrelevant details and information, litigants should be as insightful and concise as possible. Given that the importance of capturing the attention of the members of the tribunal is crucial to the successful resolution of the dispute.

The message must be presented with the receiver in mind.

➔ It is extremely important that, as storytellers, we know to whom we are going to address our pleadings; since both the judge and the popular jury are identified and obey different conceptions, our story should be tailored according to whom we have to address our initial allegations:

- ❖ *A technical judge is much more interested in dealing with the law and case law.*
- ❖ *Whereas the popular jury focuses its interest on the facts, they are the ones who retain common sense.*

It is also worth saying that we must present to the court who the characters are, what the conflict is, and the solution we intend for the judge to adopt. However, in order for the judge to identify with the party we are representing and agree with us in the resolution of the conflict, we need to use persuasion; in other words, **we need to talk about emotions.**

And this can be done in the following way:

- ➢ Presentation of the life history of our assisted person
- ➢ The way he has gone through the conflict and how it has impacted the development of his life.
- ➢ Emphasizing or highlighting in the trial the key emotions to achieve a connection with the court so that they can empathize with our side.
- ➢ Also, the implementation of logical resources (hence the importance of knowing the addressee of our message), talking about the facts, their verification or refutation, in scientific and demonstrable terms. For example, instead of basing my theory of the case on testimonial evidence, I can base it on expert evidence; perhaps the judge is more interested in what science says about it than in what third-party witnesses say.

However, making use of emotions implies that they should be coherent and appropriate; we are not going to present a melodrama, but we will propose to recover those emotions that are common to all individuals in order to create empathy.

Mention the evidence that proves your claim.

➔ Since the opening is the moment that corresponds to the persuasive introduction of the case, each litigant must identify and refer to the specific evidence that he or she plans to present during the course of the trial to support their position or argument. This evidence may include documents, witness testimony, expert testimony, photographs, or other items that support the parties' version of events or assertions.

The inclusion of this evidence in the opening argument serves to inform the other side, the judge, and the jury of the existence of such evidence and its importance in supporting the litigant's position. This also allows the litigant to establish consistency and persuasiveness in the narrative from the beginning of the trial, generating an expectation about the evidence to be presented later.

It is important to note that although the evidence is mentioned in the opening statement, it is during the presentation of evidence that it must be formally presented and admitted before the court in accordance with the applicable legal rules and procedures.

Do not argue about the result; do not delve into details.

→ We could say that opening statements are just a preview of the facts and the litigant's strategy, which starts a discovery process that litigants have to go through during the entire trial. Instead of arguing in depth, we must present - as mentioned above - a general description of our position, stating our main points without going into excessive detail or presenting specific evidence.

The reason behind this is to allow the other side to put forward its own version of the facts during its opening argument and thus avoid discussing details that have not yet been presented as evidence.

State the legal theory to be used by the litigant.

→ The mention of legal theory in the opening brief serves several purposes. First, it helps to establish the legal foundation and context in which the case will be developed. By identifying and presenting the legal theory, the litigant shows the judge and jury the legal basis upon which he or she will base his or her arguments.

In addition, mentioning legal theory during the opening argument serves to set expectations and guide the trial participants' attention to relevant legal principles. This helps focus the discussion and facilitates understanding of the litigant's position and strategy.

It should also address and anticipate weaknesses in the case.

→ It is a strategic decision, and we will do it as long as its mention is not to our detriment. With it, we will gain credibility. By mentioning our own weaknesses, we will ensure that the opposing party will not be able to show them to the court and thus further disadvantage our case.

The Power of Preparation in the **Opening Argument**

Litigant's Obligations

How a solid strategy makes the difference in your case

1. 1 Presentation of the view of the facts

- Describe the events, characters, and conflict.
- Accompany with evidence to support the perspective.

2. 1 Handling of test details

- Avoid exhaustive details in the test announcement.
- Keep the mystery to solve during the trial.

3. 1 Thesis citation

- It should be introduced at the beginning and reinforced at the end.
- Crucial to express the motto and anchor it in the court's mind.

4. 1 Do not read

Avoid reading to demonstrate readiness and confidence.

5. 1 Enhancing emotions

Capture attention from the beginning and keep it.

6. 1 What NOT to do?

➢ Be tedious: Avoid falling into monotony.
➢ Bore: Keep the presentation interesting.
➢ Delve into details: Save details for the development of the trial.

The opposing parties and their roles

In his opening statement, the prosecuting attorney or prosecutor will have to say who he is bringing to trial and what crime he is accused of. He will present his version of the facts and state the evidence he plans to present during the trial to prove the defendant's guilt.

It will also highlight the key elements of the crime and explain how they plan to establish them through testimony and evidence.

It also has the duty to state that it respects the **principle of presumption of innocence** and that it will prove that the accused **is guilty beyond a reasonable doubt.**

In the same way, he will explain the legal theory he will use to achieve his objective of guilt.

On the other hand, **the defense attorney** will use his opening argument to introduce his version of the facts and may approach two types of defense depending on his strategy:

In the **passive strategy**, it should emphasize to the members of the jury and the court, first of all, **the** validity of the presumption of innocence and highlight any relevant information that may benefit the defendant. Thus, it should be mentioned that it is the prosecution that has the burden of proof and exposes the possible weaknesses of the prosecution seeking to generate doubts regarding several aspects:

- ➢ *the legal theory of the prosecution,*
- ➢ *the way in which the facts are presented,*
- ➢ *that the accused participated in these events,*
- ➢ *that such action is prosecutable ex officio,*
- ➢ *or doubts about the defendant's ability to commit the crime.*

After all, the litigant seeks to create a reasonable doubt in the judge regarding the manner in which the prosecutor has presented his version of the facts.

In contrast, you can also establish an **active strategy** by presenting an alternative case theory to test, where you will have to highlight the slogan of your case and play a peer-to-peer role.

In this way, the litigant will present his own hypothesis by reworking the sequence of events to counter the prosecution's theory of the case, which, at the same time, obliges him to carry out a vast and effective investigation, allowing him to support his version and present a solid theory of the case to the court.

Let us remember that in the briefing, each litigant must also meet additional requirements no less important for his success in the courtroom – we have already discussed them above, but they need to be emphasized because they are essential to his role as a lead litigant and directly influence the outcome of his opening argument :

- ➢ The litigant must be sure to make a good first impression.
- ➢ Make your case persuasive and convincing.
- ➢ Make use of body language to transmit security and conviction in order to request the person who has the duty to resolve the matter to comply with the transcendental role of rendering justice in the specific case.

Structure of the opening statement

Oral litigation maxim 7: "Start with what's important." The first and last 30-second technique

Every message, even in the forensic field, must be designed in such a way that the people we are addressing want to hear it because it is something important.

Do not waste this opportunity with detours, digressions, lack of certainty when speaking, hypotheses and theories, or suspicions that are not relevant.

The people who are listening to you need certainty to solve a key issue, and you are there to give it to them.

The following is the structure used by the most successful lawyers in the United States. I hope it will also give you excellent results.

1. Say the essentials in the first 30 seconds. Include the slogan of your case. What are the most relevant needs to be included to capture attention.
2. The story: What is the problem to be solved: here, focus on answering the when and where (orient them to the scene), what (talk about the main events), why (the motives), how (explain the event covering preparation, planning, and execution), who said (the ability of witnesses), certainties (how we will support the request and why it is plausible that it happened).
3. The options that the opponent will try to test.
4. The legal effects, liability, attribution, etc.
5. Legal remedies.
6. Conclusion of the presentation in 30 seconds of message.

First of all, remembering what has been said so far, the opening argument is essential because it is the first opportunity for the litigant to speak about his case. It is, therefore, the perfect occasion to make **a good first impression.** For, in a very underlying way, the first impact or impression that the litigant is able to leave in the mind of the judge or jury will tell them what to expect from the litigant and will play a fundamental role thereafter.

A very simple way to make an easy-to-understand case is to do it in chronological order and quickly answer the six questions (which we discussed extensively in the chapter on the Theory of the case): who, how, when, where, why, and to whom?

It is advisable to use the **slogan** I have selected for my case as the introduction to my opening statement so that my thesis is anchored in the minds of the members of the tribunal. In this way, I fly my flag at the same time as I make the case for the values that need to be rescued or the feelings that need to be protected. **I unite the slogan with my theory of the case.**

At the same time, in the trial, it is not only important what I say but how I say it. My story may well be very coherent, but if the audience does not trust what I say and if they do not take my version as true, it is of no use. That is why it is necessary that we develop leadership skills; a leading lawyer is able to win over the members of the courtroom with impeccable verbal and body language.

There are many ways to make a persuasive plea, but the first thing to keep in mind -and I emphasize this- is who will be the addressee of my message; only then will I tailor my presentation to the needs and characteristics of that addressee in order to achieve my objectives.

But what to do in case the court where I have to litigate is not used to it, or if the procedural rules of my city do not provide for this litigation technique?

In these cases, what I suggest you do is ask for it as a leader and lead the way. For example: "Excuse me, Mr. Presiding Judge, I need to state my case through opening arguments so that you understand what our position is going to be throughout the trial." It is likely that, with good reasoning, that request will be granted.

Refer to the evidence to be submitted retrospectively

After duly stating the facts, we must make mention of the evidence that we will bring later to the trial; that is to say, it is not enough with the mere enunciation made by the litigant, but he must prove that what he says is true. Otherwise, he will incur a falsehood, which may be a cause of disappointment for the members of the court.

When litigants announce the evidence that we will use to support our position, we should not go into detail. Remember that the evidence is a discovery that we have to unveil throughout the trial. It is enough just to mention the evidence we will use to prove a certain fact and what result we expect to obtain. However, always bear in mind that this statement must be true and demonstrable.

Approach to the legal theory on which the thesis is based

After describing his view of the facts and mentioning the evidence, the litigant proceeds to present the legal basis for his theory with the sole purpose of indicating that the context and the aspects required to acquit or convict the accused are present.

One can even mention the dispute that exists between the defense's accusation and our legal position to give an example.

The petition

The litigant is about to conclude his pleadings, so he will ask the judge to evaluate the facts he has presented in order to rule in favor of his client. In other words, he will ask for the defendant to be convicted or acquitted.

Conclusion

To close the opening statement, we must anticipate our weaknesses and mention our motto again.

Steps to follow for the preparation of the Opening Argument

1. ***Exhaustive review of the facts***
   → *Analyze and understand the details of the case*
   → *Identify key elements and relevant circumstances*
2. ***Research and evidence-gathering***
   → *Review available evidence, including documents, testimony, experts, etc.*
   → *Select the most convincing and relevant evidence to support the argument.*
3. ***Define the purpose of the opening statement***
   → *Establish the main purpose of the pleading: to persuade, inform, generate empathy, etc.*
   → *Identify the position and theory of the case to be presented to the jury.*
4. ***Development of a clear and logical structure***
   → *Organize the relevant aspects in a coherent sequence.*
   → *Establish an impactful introduction and a convincing conclusion.*
5. ***Creating a powerful narrative***
   → *Build an engaging story that connects emotionally with the audience.*
   → *Use metaphors, analogies, or examples to reinforce arguments.*
6. ***Practicing and polishing the opening statement***
   → *Conduct rehearsals to perfect language, tone, and fluency.*
   → *Make adjustments based on feedback received and internal feedback.*
7. ***Adapt the pleading to the audience and context.***
   → *Consider the characteristics of the jury and/or judge*
   → *Tailoring language and arguments to maximize impact.*
8. ***Establishing an effective visual presentation***
   → *Use visual aids such as slides, graphics, or videos if appropriate*
   → *Design a clear and attractive presentation that reinforces the key points.*
9. ***Preparing for possible setbacks***
   → *Anticipate opposing questions or arguments and be prepared to respond.*
   → *Be aware of possible objections and how to deal with them effectively.*

Why is it important to make an opening statement?

It gives the judge the tools to resolve justice disputes and objections.

→ It establishes the position in the trial and the evidence with which the litigant will handle it.

→ It leaves the judge with knowledge of each litigant's position, what their theory of the case will be, and how they will defend it.

→ Determines the **relevance** of each of the allegations of the evidence to be presented at trial, thus being able to resolve the various disputes that arise.

PROFESSIONAL ADVICE

- ★ *Use a firm, confident tone as you begin your opening statement. Create a powerful statement that captures the audience's attention and establishes the importance of the case.*
- ★ *Use clear and concise language to facilitate jurors' understanding and keep their attention.*
- ★ *List the witnesses and evidence you will present at trial. Highlight their relevance and how they support your theory of the case. This will help the judge and members of the court understand the importance of the evidence to be presented.*
- ★ *Use strong and convincing arguments to support your theory of the case. Emphasize the strength of your evidence and refute possible defense arguments. Make your presentation clear and coherent.*
- ★ *End your opening statement with a powerful closing that reinforces your position and calls for justice.*

➔ Establishes the scope of relevance of the entire test.

THE CASE RESTS ON THE DIRECT EXAMINATION OF WITNESSES

"Testimonial evidence is at the heart of the case and of the work. On the litigants depends the success of their results."

D.H.

Evidentiary stage:

"Things by their name."

After the pleadings were presented, the judge loudly stated that the ***victim*** *should testify.*

- Mrs. Martina Ramirez, go ahead and sit down. I warn you that the Penal Code punishes those who lie in court and aggravates the penalty when such falsehood is to the detriment of the accused; I ask you, Mrs. Ramirez: do you swear or promise to tell the truth?

- Yes, I swear," Martina answered, and then she began to answer the questions that were put to her.

Well, this term used by the magistrate when addressing the complainant/witness as the victim had already marked the fate of the process by virtue of the fact that such denomination should occur as long as it is demonstrated that the facts asserted by the accusing party are corroborated by the evidence rendered in the case. In other words, procedurally speaking, the judge should wait until the trial is over to establish with rigor of truth that the person who was indicated as the victim was really the victim and that the victimizer is the person being prosecuted. Respecting the presumption of innocence demands it.

However, treating it as such at the beginning of the process, when there are only statements without corroboration, leads, in the great majority of cases, to twisting the rules governing procedural activity and committing errors to the detriment of the parties.

It is clear that if we treat the complainant as a victim, we are ensuring that the other party is the victimizer, and this clearly undermines the state of innocence that every person accused of a crime should enjoy. This state should only cease when there is a final sentence that establishes his guilt.

In the real case that I share as an example, this bias on the part of the magistrate caused Martina to be allowed to add information never previously mentioned in any of the dozens of complaints made against her ex-husband, that we were deprived of the possibility of a proper confrontation, that the supposed treating psychologist was subpoenaed, at the time of the facts denounced, when according to the evidence gathered in the case, Martina had maintained that she was not in therapy at that time, and worse still, the accusing parties (neither public nor private) had offered the mentioned psychologist as a witness in the stages intended for that purpose. All of which was done outside the procedural deadlines established for that purpose.

In addition, and as if that were not enough, new facts were allowed to be incorporated (outside those that constituted the object of the proceedings), obviously more and more burdensome, which finally caused an alteration of the factual basis and, therefore of the accusation, all of this while the trial was in progress.

Does this story sound familiar?

Although, as a teacher, I seek to inspire my colleagues to make positive changes within their community, I cannot help but recognize as a litigator that these problems are present more than ever and that we must bring them to light to create awareness of the harm that is committed when judicial guarantees are violated, depriving the entire community of the legal certainty that should be provided.

Hence the importance of a certain rigorousness that should be demanded of judicial operators. The judge should have called Martina to the stand to testify as a complainant/witness and not as a victim, at least to preserve a certain image of impartiality, which is due to all of us who come to the process in search of justice.

At present, the administration of justice is going through a series of conflicts that, in my opinion, it does not know how to manage. An example of this is that without any legal certainty whatsoever (since the evidentiary stage has just begun) and given that universal procedural principles are in force (the presumption of innocence is one of the most important), judges are calling victims those who up to now have been plaintiffs demanding justice.

This detail makes a dent in the whole procedural issue by virtue of the fact that the judge reveals his position in that trial.

It does not take a very astute person to understand that if it is the judge himself who uses the word victim when mentioning the complainant, as a logical consequence of this, whoever is on the other side, in the dock, is undoubtedly her victimizer.

And if there is no room for doubt, the question is why do we conduct a whole trial under the paradigm of an accusatory system when, as the reader can appreciate, we are clearly facing an inquisitorial process. It was established that someone is a victim (without evidence because it has not yet been produced).

In short, what I seek through this example, which I have seen dozens of times both when it is my turn to represent the "victim" as well as the accused, is to raise awareness in judicial operators so that we really get fully into the culture of the adversarial process, leaving behind phrases and practices that are inquisitorial even if we ignore it.

In the chapter where we addressed the opening statement, we made it clear that,

What the lawyers have alleged is not evidence; it is their statements about what happened and how they intend to prove it. Their function is to position the judges or jurors to understand what they are about to witness next. Therefore, if the witness does not express what the litigant has announced, he or she will not be proving his or her theory and will probably lose the case. Judges should be attentive to this detail so as not to give the victory to those who simply have the facility of oratory, express themselves convincingly, but fail to prove anything they had promised.

Within the process, it is useful to state that not just any person can go to testify at the trial; he/she must meet an essential condition: to have relevant information that allows the judge to discover the truth about what happened. He may have witnessed the facts that are the subject of the confrontation, know the parties involved, or perhaps have knowledge of some relevant information. I clarify this because many litigants believe that if more witnesses are summoned, it is better; however, this is a serious mistake.

With this caveat, people and judges get upset when they realize that they are wasting their time. Listening to someone who has only hearsay to contribute or so much confusion that it really adds or subtracts nothing for the parties to the dispute. Thinking ahead and offering witnesses responsibly is the key to maximizing trial performance.

Then they are witnesses:

Those persons who have directly perceived, either by sight, hearing, touch, and/or smell, a fact that is the subject of investigation in the process. When the litigant offers a witness, he does so only because it corresponds to and supports his theory of the case. This is so because as there is no theory of the judge's case, there are no court witnesses either, but witnesses that are offered by the parties. The same thing that happens in the civil process happens in the criminal process. The judge does not know who can provide information; it is the parties who tell him who they are and establish their usefulness for the clarification of the facts.

Witnesses play an important role in the judicial process; they are capable of offering us the slogan or theme that we are going to state in the trial, of accrediting or discrediting a certain position or thesis, and they can even have the ability to make us win or lose the case.

A requirement of the accusatory process.

As we have pointed out in previous chapters, the adversarial accusatory process requires that both the judge and the jury have no knowledge of the conflict until they are present in the courtroom in order to hear the explanation of the facts from each litigant, who have the duty to discover, as the process progresses, the truth they are defending and proving their theory of the case by means of convincing evidence.

In order to take full advantage of this opportunity provided by direct examination, it is important for litigators to set clear objectives to carry out this technique. In other words, we must know what we want to achieve with our witness and devise a strategic plan accordingly.

Asking questions is an art requiring planning, method, and technique, on whose skill will depend on whether this key piece of information is extracted for our case.

In this sense, after having conducted an investigation with determination and responsibility, and in order to fulfill the objectives we have set, we will bring our witness to the stand **to obtain from him or her that extract of information that he or she has to support our factual propositions.**

The quintessence of direct examination is that the information - which every witness has - must be discovered by the litigants through the right questions; that is how it will be the declarants who will tell the members of the courtroom how the facts were, it will then be a reconstruction of the story made by the litigant through the witness and, of course, driven by the assertiveness of his or her questions.

Getting a witness to talk seems like a simple task, but the truth is that bringing the witness into the field of action requires the very refined skill of the litigator.

I always tell my students - and as common law teaches us - that testimonial evidence "is the heart of the case." It is the marrow and the vital pulse of our case, as it stands as the irreplaceable occasion for litigants to prove everything we announced in the opening argument.

So, it will depend on our interrogation skills whether they remain vigorous or fade away. **Our duty is none other than to drive it with energy, vitality, and strength to achieve the objectives.**

Objectives of direct questioning

What is the ideal of direct questioning?

Witnesses are the ones who provide, most of the time, the most substantial and controversial information for a case. All the people who have witnessed an event have different versions of what happened, and it is important that we get to know them all in order to discover our strengths and weaknesses.

Oral Litigation Maxim 7: *What was not proven at trial does not exist.*

That is to say that you can have an ambitious theory of the case supported by an exhaustive investigation, but... if, when applying the technique, you do not manage to extract those exact words from the witness's mouth, that will allow the judge to form an idea of what happened according to your version. The story will not be written, and therefore, this information gap cannot be filled in other stages.

This is really about making every effort to achieve something very big. Below, we analyze the main aspects to be considered by the litigant.

1. **First objective:** **The presentation of the witness**

Why are we bringing this witness to testify?

As we have stated from the beginning of this section, the idea of calling a witness to the stand is because the story he will present through his testimony is functional to our theory of the case.

➔ Then, we will start with the question: who is the witness?

His or her role in the trial will be strongly connected to who he or she is as a person.

➔ I have to introduce him, and for that, I first have to get to know him.

Undoubtedly, when offering a witness, we have a duty to know his or her history in depth. For example, his address, occupation (where he lives or works), whether he is married or single, whether he has a family and children. Gathering all this information will allow us to understand him better and develop some empathy with him.

Now that we have completed our investigation and selected our witnesses, let's focus on being very clear about what we want to obtain from the witness. That is, what portion of the information do we need to prove our factual propositions – to support our legal framework? So, the first thing we will do is to talk about the witness, introduce him/her through questions, and he/she will tell the courtroom, through his/her answers, who he/she is in order to establish his/her credibility and honorability.

2. **Second objective:** **The accreditation of its veracity and objectivity.**

The importance of providing quality information about the witness

Once we have passed the stage of finding out who the witness is and the reasons why the witness should be believed, we will enter the second stage, where we will deal with the **conditions of perception.** In this stage, we will talk about the aspects that may affect the perception of the witness and, at the same time, the perception that the judge and the jury have about him.

To fulfill this purpose, we must provide valuable information to the judges and jury to ensure the credibility of the witness and, therefore, that of his or her testimony.

Likewise, we will inquire if he has knowledge of the parties: if he is a friend or foe, if he knows the parties, and when he knows them if he is a creditor or debtor. What is known as the generalities of the law to demonstrate that in the case of knowing the parties, this will not affect his testimony or the veracity of his statements.

The accreditation of factual propositions

The third step – and the third objective of the direct examination technique – is to verify the factual propositions.

In this sense, we should not go directly to the facts, but in a detailed way, we will break down the story, and according to this, we will carry out the interrogation from a general perspective to a more detailed one; that is to say, to start from the general to the concrete in order to reconstruct our narration.

Regarding the presentation of this narrative, there are two ways of presenting it: thematically or chronologically. However, the general recommendation and practice is to present it chronologically in order for the judge to understand the sequence of events more clearly. Hence, from the questions we ask the witness, we will narrate our story in a clear and simple way so that it remains in the judge's memory and in the memory of the members of the court.

Once we have stated the facts, we will highlight the most important events of our story through a series of questions that allow us to situate the *what, how, when, where, why, to whom,* and then *what happened*; we will use these to tell the story, with special emphasis on the details that we need to bring to light.

And if possible, we include a special touch that consists of extracting feelings, emotions, and personal perceptions from the witness to form a chapter of the story that will remain engraved in the psyche of the judge and the jury.

What specific objectives does the lead litigator seek to achieve in direct examination?

How leadership enables litigators to approach and manage the technique of direct examination of witnesses.

> *The main objective that a leading litigator should pursue in applying the technique is to demonstrate to the judge/jury that he/she is the best person to discover and make known the truth of the facts.*

In this way, he will strengthen the credibility gained in the opening statement, which will allow him to continue telling the story, but this time through the words of the witness.

As we have seen since the beginning of this book, the current legal world requires from the litigator a new perspective and a new perspective. Thus, as my method proposes, the leading litigator will be the one who conducts the interrogation with conviction and is oriented to the objectives that should have been set beforehand, of course.

As a result, the witness becomes the architect of the story to be told in the testimony. He is not the protagonist; he **is the one who constructs the narrative through the voice of the witness.** In this way, he manages to express his leadership skills since he is in charge of channeling the interrogation with the purpose of rescuing those values that constitute the basis of his thesis and that he tries to extol and raise as his banner, making the judge and the members of the jury adopt his position.

Litigator's deficit: If you don't know how to ask questions, you could lose your case.

It is not only about knowing how to ask open-ended questions but also about asking questions following your plan. Extracting fragments of information from each question is a key detail in setting the course of your case.

Many times, there are litigants who justify themselves by saying that the witness did not tell such and such a thing, that he or she did not testify to it. However, it is important to emphasize when the information does not come from the witness; it is more a matter of a deficit of the litigant than of the witness himself; that is to say, it often happens that the lawyer did not know how to cross-examine.

Generally, this failure is linked to a lack of research, doubts about the information to be reproduced, lack of preparation of the witness, sloppiness in the handling of techniques, or inexperience.

These problems of the litigant can be noticed in the middle of the trial when their questions are confusing, and the witness is unable to understand them. Also, they can be ambiguous; that is, he asks two things at the same time, and the witness evades or answers only one. Or because -perhaps- he did not ask what he should have asked. Also, it happens that the litigant asked suggestive questions that the opposing party objected to, and the litigant was not prepared to rephrase. In other words, he asked the question, but the witness was not allowed to answer.

In short, the litigator's leadership will be reflected in his or her mastery to successfully conduct the cross-examination and redeem the values that have been severed, thereby consolidating his or her theory of the case and persuading his or her audience.

The second objective is due to his work as a strategist and his expertise to act in accordance with his goal. In other words, with a well-defined plan in hand - previously elaborated- that allows him to establish a clear objective. After announcing this plan in the initial pleadings, in his opening, it is the interrogation or direct examination when the litigant begins to execute that plan.

This means that in the pursuit of this objective, the litigant must be very clear about why he is summoning his witness, what information he wishes to obtain, and what steps he must follow in order not to deviate from the plan he has drawn up.

Remember at all times that the litigant's statements are not evidence.

A litigator who assumes and puts into practice the new skills required by the oral system of litigation knows that he or she must tell the facts through his or her witnesses. For what he or she says in the opening argument is not evidence, therefore he or she must back up his or her thesis with what the witness will say.

He knows that in order to do so, he must ask the right questions that make the witness say "the magic words," that is to say, that the questions that the litigant directs to his witness will be the key to obtaining that fragment of the story that serves to prove his theory, to prove that the facts are as he presented them at the beginning of the trial.

In this sense, the witness will tell – what the litigant wants and knows he will tell because he so arranged – the reconstruction of the factual propositions with such persuasiveness that the members of the court are inclined to adopt the theory of the case that the litigant offered.

This **new litigant** we have been talking about throughout these pages understands that the trial is not a trial to be investigated. Investigation is a mandatory pre-trial task that must be undertaken by any lawyer who is committed to his or her fundamental purpose: to win. As a result, before he or she begins to guide the direct examination, he or she knows what the witness will answer because he or she has thoroughly studied every element of your case.

For this purpose, you should not ask questions you do not know the answer to.

Otherwise, he would leave his fate to chance. Let us remember that the witness – with the guidance of the litigant – must say as persuasively as possible what serves the cause defended by the summoning party.

The role of the intervening parties in the process of accreditation of testimonial evidence

On the judge's performance

> *The judge does not go to the oral trial to investigate the truth.*

Unlike the inquisitorial system and the mixed system, the adversarial accusatory system requires the judge to maintain a passive role -that is, he or she does not question witnesses- in order to maintain objectivity and bias in his or her decisions.

When a witness is brought before the bench, the judge:

- He shall take the oath of the witness to warn him of the penalties for false testimony.
- He is also obliged to act when false testimony is committed in his presence.
- Exceptionally, he/she may ask clarifying questions directly to the witness.
- He conducts the hearing of the oral debate, is the director of the process, and settles the different disputes that may arise between the parties. It resolves minor disputes and objections, always maintaining its role of impartiality.

→ Procedural guarantees to be safeguarded

In the adversarial system, as we understand it, the judge enters the courtroom with a basic understanding of the positions of the parties without detailed knowledge of the facts at issue. **His or her role is not to investigate or question the veracity of the facts but rather to administer justice impartially from a neutral perspective.**

In other words, **its function is limited to obtaining information, processing it to the best of its knowledge and belief, and then resolving it.** However, there are certain questions that are authorized for their investiture, for example, clarifying questions: when the litigant questioning the witness leaves empty spaces that the judge needs to be able to fill in; in this case, he must limit his question to simply obtain that missing portion of information, but cannot go beyond that.

At trial, **the onus is on the litigants to rely on witnesses to present the evidence and relate the details of the material evidence through their testimony.** In other words, in this legal system, information is required to be presented by the direct source, who must present all his knowledge before the judge. In the adversarial accusatory process, **the judge is forbidden the power to investigate.** And, unlike the systems that preceded it, the accusation is not equivalent to a conviction, but the witnesses are required to come to the trial in order to achieve due contradiction. Cross-examination strategies show us that the less involved a judge is and the more impartial he or she remains, the fairer the trial will be, as litigants will have greater freedom to develop and execute their strategies.

The performance of litigants, in general

At the time of the testimonial hearing, the attorney has complete autonomy to execute his strategy and call the witnesses he deems most appropriate and in accordance with his theory of the case. It is the litigator's responsibility to select competent witnesses. In addition, the question arises: **What questions will you ask during the testimony?**

→ Safeguarding of due process in the specific case

Sometimes, litigants do not perform their work adequately, leaving gaps or ambiguities to the detriment of the accused. In such situations, the judge is obliged – in good faith – to assume that role, ask questions, and inquire into the facts. However, this compromises and tarnishes his impartiality, one of the fundamental principles of the adversarial process.

In this situation, it is appropriate to summon the litigants to the stand and inquire about the time each has had to prepare his or her case and even consider adjourning the hearing. Also, the litigants may request an extension of time if so required.

Therefore, it is crucial to emphasize that lack of preparation, however minimal, can compromise our theory of the case and put it at risk.

In the event that the judge perceives that the litigant is not committed to the theory of the case, the trial should be suspended, and the party should be asked to appoint a new advocate. Failure to do so risks an erroneous ruling and, as a result, a wrongful conviction.

→ Rights it represents and how they are carried out

Counsel's investiture during oral argument hearings gives him the freedom to present whatever evidence he deems necessary to support his theory of the case. In this regard, he or she may select the witnesses he or she wishes to bring to trial and ask pertinent questions. In addition, unlike the previous system, trial attorneys are responsible for the theory of the case, which gives them the freedom to waive a witness if he or she is not helpful or if what he or she was going to prove is not relevant.

On the other hand, the litigant also has the right to cross-examine the witnesses presented by the opposing party. This implies the power to generate controversy during the oral hearing and to protect his own witness from any hostile behavior on the part of the adversary.

It is important to emphasize that the litigant, as guarantor and watchdog of compliance with procedural rules and constitutional guarantees, may make motions to ensure the proper conduct of the oral trial and achieve the proposed objectives.

In summary, the lawyer in oral argument hearings can and should:

- submit evidence,
- select witnesses,
- cross-examine the opposing party, and
- ensure compliance with procedural rules and guarantees.

→ Previous interviews and their objectives

At this point, let's back up a bit and analyze the role of the litigator before the oral trial. It is crucial to understand that a lawyer's work is not limited to public hearings. There are pre-trial tasks that must be performed to avoid surprises and to ensure that the facts are presented as we have announced them. During the opening phase, it is critical to be clear about what we want to prove and how we will prove it. This is where oral litigation techniques come into play, allowing the litigant to interview witnesses prior to the hearing.

However, there are cases in which some lawyers resort to dishonest practices. What exactly does this involve? It involves interviewing the witness and providing him/her with additional information that has not been corroborated, with the aim of enhancing his/her testimony and knowledge of the facts and personal circumstances when, in fact, he/she does not possess them. This dishonest conduct is against the codes of ethics governing the legal profession in all countries of the world.

It is essential to preserve the principle of equality before the law and equality of arms and to gain society's trust in our work. We cannot resort to false witnesses to obtain a victory in a case. In addition to damaging our reputation, we expose ourselves to sanctions and put at serious risk those who are willing to testify falsely in an oral trial.

> *I can never be a good lawyer if I need to rely on false evidence to win a case.*

Justice is a serious matter, and we must approach it as such. Behind every case, there are interests and rights that we lawyers are obliged to protect for the sake of a system of social cooperation.

On the performance of the witness

Having taken these initial considerations and preliminary remarks into account, we will now turn to the different interviews that an attorney may conduct with a witness prior to trial.

These interviews may involve direct witnesses or professionals such as police or experts present during the events. In this context, the lawyer assumes the role of investigator, whose main objective is to obtain as much information as possible about the facts before the trial in order to build his theory of the case in a conscious and solid manner.

Order and scheduling of witness statements

Not only will we conduct direct examinations to support my case, but I can also address any weaknesses I deem pertinent, as long as they do not affect my theory or the credibility of the witness.

This will allow me to control the narrative of the story during cross-examination, preventing the witness's weaknesses from portraying him or her as unreliable or withholding information. An effective strategy is to address the weaknesses with the witness himself, making sure to maintain control and not allowing these weaknesses to prejudice my legal argument. In this regard, questions will focus on his or her personal knowledge of the people involved in the conflict.

External order

Order of presentation of our testimonial evidence

When it comes to strategically planning the presentation of testimonial evidence, it is crucial to consider how to make an impact from the outset. This involves carefully selecting the strongest witnesses to present at the beginning and end of the process. In the initial phase, it is advisable to present witnesses who provide strong evidence about the facts in question. Then, in the final stage, witnesses capable of generating an emotional impact, appealing to feelings, and creating a deep commitment to the cause should be included.

For example, if we have a complex case involving multiple raids and various investigations of different defendants, presenting all the information chronologically may make it difficult for both the judge and the jury to understand. Instead, the appropriate strategy would be to organize the presentation into thematic or investigative blocks, grouping the witnesses related to each specific block.

In this way, we were able to subpoena the relevant witnesses in relation to each piece of information, facilitating a clear and orderly understanding of the case for all those involved in the legal process.

The main objective is for the story to be understandably persuasive.

Regarding the organization of the witness statement, it is crucial to carefully consider the order in which the witnesses will be presented. It is necessary to evaluate which of them will allow the introduction of the material evidence at the most opportune moment to achieve the desired impact. In addition, the appropriate time to introduce the expert witnesses must be considered.

In criminal cases, it is common to begin by quoting the victim, as this person can provide a chronological account of the events and convey the emotions and feelings experienced, which generates a great impression on both judges and members of the court.

Secondly, the physician who attended to the victim could be introduced, who can discuss the injuries sustained, their duration, and whether they are permanent or temporary. In addition, the physician may describe the victim's emotional state during the medical examination, whether she was in shock, emotional, or beaten. He or she may also refer to a diagnosis made, relevant expert reports, or medical records.

Third, the police officer who found the victim running desperately in the street, asking for help, can be quoted. This will help to illustrate the moment of his intervention and the situation in which the victim found herself.

Subsequently, witnesses who saw the victim in such conditions or those who observed the perpetrator fleeing may be cited.

It is essential to carefully plan and consider the order of presentation of witnesses and material evidence in order to maximize impact and persuasiveness in court.

Types of questions that can be asked in direct questioning

> *The lawyer must never lose the*
> *control over your case*

➔ Narrative type questions

Narrative questions, which require an extensive amount of information, used to be common in the old system. However, these questions demonstrate a lack of preparation on the part of trial counsel, as they leave too much latitude for the witness to answer. Instead of acting as a director or leader, the attorney allows the witness to answer in an open-ended manner, which increases the risk that his or her answers will not fit the theory of the case. Using this type of questioning is not recommended, as it can result in a loss of control over the case.

➔ Open-ended questions

Open-ended questions are those that are posed to the witness with the objective of obtaining more detailed answers. Some classic examples of open-ended questions include: what happened, how it happened, when it happened, where it took place, and why it happened. Although there are many other variations, these are the most common.

These questions provide the witness with a sense of direction and often generate a fluid dialogue. In this type of interaction, the witness becomes the protagonist of the story, while the trial attorney assumes the role of the conductor.

➔ Closed questions

Closed-ended questions are used when specific and detailed information is needed. These questions are ideal for obtaining precise details and can be used to typify or delegitimize behavior. For example, we might ask, *"What was the color of the car in which you noted the perpetrator's license plate?"* or *"How many bottles of alcohol did you find in the trunk of the said car?"*

We can also probe for the location of the murder weapon with questions such as, "Where exactly was the murder weapon?" In this way, by using close-ended questions, we seek to narrow the information to obtain specific details that we might not otherwise obtain.

➔ Suggestive questions

Leading questions, although not contemplated in some procedural codes, are prohibited on direct examination under U.S. Federal Rule 611-B. It is considered malpractice to use these types of questions, as they place the attorney in the spotlight rather than the facts.

An example of this type of question is: *"You were located 20 meters from the scene, and there were 5 people in front of you at the time.* From your position, *couldn't you have seen the other witness when he was called by the police?"*

These questions are subjective and allow only yes or no answers.

The litigant and body language in oral proceedings

At the climax of this crucial analysis of this litigation technique, we are at the point of drawing conclusions that will make our oral argument efficient. As I emphasized in my opening argument, the presentation of the theory of the case is analogous to a literary table of contents or a movie trailer, underscoring the importance of addressing each chapter with precision through deposition testimony.

Meticulous preparation is essential to succeed in oral hearings, which proceed at a dizzying pace, with no room for improvisation. In the face of this challenge, the key lies in processing the necessary information in advance, stressing the importance of structuring witness statements in thematic order to deal with the spontaneity inherent in direct examination.

In this situation, it is important to remember that the lawyer does not have the leading role during direct examination; this role is occupied by the witness. The ability to express emotions and bring out crucial issues depends to a great extent on the attention paid to the witness's body language, whose first impression is comparable in relevance to that of the lawyer himself.

Proper treatment of the witness emerges as an inescapable facet of the development of justice. All too often, the witness is subjected to disdain, whether during the pretrial phase or at the hearing itself. Nevertheless, their role is transcendental to the fulfillment of justice; without witnesses, there is no evidence, no case, no justice. Ergo, respect, and consideration for the witness stand as an unshakable foundation.

As for the work of the litigator, it is necessary not to conceive his role merely as that of throwing witnesses into the void of the oral trial. The responsibility lies in caring for and valuing the role of the witness, protecting him or her from possible misconduct on the part of the adversary. The elaboration of clear witness statements, the consideration of the witness' time, and the application of comprehensible questions are unavoidable guidelines.

The emotional management of the litigant during cross-examination is vital to the success of the case: the ability to control the pace, modulate the voice according to the needs, and maintain self-control are invaluable skills. In exceptional situations that make this emotional control difficult, it is a lawyer's duty to notify the judge to request the interruption or adjustment of the hearing. Awareness of our humanity and anticipation through thorough preparation are the pillars that will ensure the strength of our performance at trial.

PROFESSIONAL ADVICE

Recommendations for questioning a witness:

★ *We must work with planning and organization of information well in advance of the oral hearing.*

★ *Establish with which witnesses we can prove the facts, the most important elements of our thesis; to do this, we will start with the best witnesses and also end with the best ones. This way, the information is recorded for the judge in case they intervene.*

★ *Organize the questions chronologically, and in this way, we introduce information about the facts in an escalating manner, which allows the judge to have global knowledge about the case.*

★ *Organize the questions thematically, this is especially useful in cases of complex crimes or when several raids have been conducted. Approach the witness, keeping in mind what specific information I want that witness to give me.*

★ *Finally, if we find ourselves in the position of having a star witness for our case, it is very important to think strategically about at what point I will call him or her to the stand before and after other witnesses.*

DIRECT EXAMINATION OF EXPERTS

Let us help the judge to give scientific support to the resolution of the matter.

Expert evidence is the framework of the case; when it is present, it orients the judge and gives him/her security due to its scientific support to the resolutions reached. In this sense, it is much more complex for litigants to question the grounds of a judgment when they are based on expert evidence.

Unlike the witnesses of the fact, who have immediate experience and real knowledge about the events, the nature of which forms the issue to be elucidated, **the persons who embody the figure of the expert witness have specialized knowledge in a specific field related to the issue in question, but have not witnessed the facts.**

These experts are summoned by each party in order to give their assessment of the process and to substantiate -thanks to their highly qualified knowledge- the finding or dissent of a fact for the resolution of the case. Therefore, they will be summoned to the oral trial to provide explanations on the matter.

But what are the requirements for an expert witness to be considered valid in an oral trial?

The validity of an expert's opinion in an oral trial depends on several factors:

➔ First, it is essential that the expert witness has a solid knowledge in his or her area of expertise, supported by relevant studies, doctorates, master's degrees, or postgraduate degrees in that specific field. In other words, for an expert's voice to be valued in an oral trial, it is essential that he or she possesses solid knowledge backed by academic training or relevant experience in the field.

➔ As a second requirement, it is necessary that their participation be relevant to the resolution of the points in dispute in the case.

It is essential to emphasize that not all cases require the intervention of an expert or specialist; in fact, this is usually the exception.

*Therefore, it is necessary for the litigant to establish that the complexity or technical nature of the case **requires the participation of an expert** to provide a specialized view that contributes to the fair and accurate resolution of the facts in dispute.*

Demonstrating and ensuring that such intervention is indeed relevant and essential to unraveling the fundamental aspects of the case is crucial to obtaining the court's support and ensuring a fair and effective legal process.

In some cases, the expert may be called upon because of his or her outstanding professional experience, supported by recommendations from colleagues.

However, in an oral trial, it is essential to have tools to assess the suitability and competence of that expert or specialist.

To this end, let us return to my strategy for assuming our role as litigators. As **investigative litigators,** our task is to examine whether the case requires the involvement of an expert. So, with the file in hand:

- ➢ *we evaluate all tests,*
- ➢ *we communicate with our customer*
- ➢ *and interview witnesses.*

These actions will help us determine if the presence of a specialist is necessary to support our theory of the case.

In the adversarial system, both the prosecution and the defense conduct their own investigation. Therefore, our main mission is to identify any point of conflict that requires the intervention of an expert for clarification.

However, a question arises: of all the available specialties, which one will be the most useful for my case?

Expert witnesses can be doctors, scientists, mechanics, engineers, architects, and systems analysts, among others. Our job will be to determine which of them can help us develop our theory of the case and give it weight during the oral trial.

Expert selection analysis

As **lead counsel**, one of our responsibilities is to interview the various expert witnesses to assess their suitability and compatibility with our role as litigators and responsible for our case.

In addition, it is crucial to establish clear contract clauses that the expert must respect, including the prohibition to act against the interests of the party we represent. Building a relationship based on trust involves conducting a thorough investigation into the background and reputation of the expert in question.

As litigators who seek to obtain convincing results in favor of our objectives, we cannot run the risk of losing our credibility, and this depends – to a great extent – on the proper selection of the expert witness. Therefore, it is necessary to find a professional who fits the specific needs of the case and who is capable of resolving in the clearest manner the unknowns that arise from the facts. **Our objective is to clearly present our theory of the case to the judge and jury.**

It is worth remembering that if we choose an unsuitable expert, both our credibility and that of our client will be compromised. Therefore, it is essential to know the professional quality of the expert we are hiring, as this has a direct impact on the outcome and perception of the case.

In this sense, it is extremely important that you lead the relationship with the expert; otherwise, you could put your case at risk.

To illustrate the above, I would like to share with you a personal and professional experience.

My role in that process was to represent the parents of a girl who had been touched in her private parts by her swimming teacher. The girl was going to be interviewed by the psychologists appointed by the Prosecutor, who had the function of determining if the girl was in a condition to testify in a Gesell Chamber. Everything according to the protocols was established, so much so that I informed the parents of the need to appoint a child psychologist expert to intervene in the process, control it, and to be able to make certain requests. In addition, we could later attach the particular report if they did not agree with the result of the official report.

As part of my strategy, I offered the parents the intervention of experts I knew and whom I could ensure would perform their work according to the needs and particularities of the case. However, the parents decided to appoint an expert that I did not know, which I had to accept.

The role of the expert is fundamental, and even though they all perform their work according to the rules of their profession, art, or trade and are obliged to tell the truth, this does not mean that they cannot contribute from their approach and other points of view. However, this is not what happened.

In that initial interview, where the child was questioned about the fact that it was part of the accusation when the procedural object was totally different. The expert appointed by her parents did not act as a controller of the act and stated her opposition to the proceeding in that sense. Therefore, the expert witness endorsed that the girl be interrogated in an environment other than the Gesell chamber.

Secondly, the girl, besides being subjected to inquiries by the official experts, when asked about the facts, manifested an absolute rejection and fear of her swimming teacher, but she did not refer to facts of abuse, but violent facts. The conclusion of the official experts and the expert witness was that time had erased from the child's memory the events she had suffered, and for this reason, they recommended NOT to do the Gesell chamber.

When our expert witness told me about the result of the interview and that she had decided to endorse the official opinion, I asked her for explanations and ways to rectify that opinion, which she then did, but, as you can imagine, it was already too late.

The parents understood then because I told them about the need to form a team with the designated experts, and they regretted their decision, but this unconsulted act marked the fate of the process because even though the girl had nightmares mentioning her aggressor, even though she could put into words the vexatious acts she suffered when she was only 5 years old, the children's defender and also the prosecutor decided not to continue with the investigation, which generated impunity for this sexual aggressor and potential risk for other girls in the same situation.

My little assisted child was deprived of the right to be heard under the conditions established by law and in an adequate environment.

The intervention of this expert witness was detrimental since she did not demand that the protocols be complied with, that the right of the child to be heard in the Gesell chamber be respected, nor did she demand that the child's right to be heard be respected. Endorsing a report that is clearly arbitrary and illegal.

I hope that this case serves as an example of how we, the litigants, have to take the reins of the trial. Although we form a team with our clients, we must be aware that they are not involved in these procedural matters, so it is extremely important that they listen to those of us who are experts in the law.

In addition, it is important to emphasize the importance of the expert's prior preparation. Before he sits on the witness stand, the trial lawyer must prepare him thoroughly. The way the expert expresses himself, his gestures, and his general demeanor are aspects that the lawyer must study and take into account in order to present a solid and persuasive case.

It is also necessary to clarify that recommendations from other attorney colleagues do not guarantee that an expert will be useful for our particular case. Each case is unique, so we need to carefully evaluate the expert's skills, knowledge, and experience to ensure that he or she is the most appropriate for our specific case.

Incidentally, as strategic lawyers, we must think ahead and plan our actions to address various possibilities and complications that may arise during trial. This will allow us to respond effectively to the challenges that arise, thus ensuring strong and effective legal representation.

Being **strategic lawyers will help** us to collaborate effectively with the expert witness to achieve our objectives. However, it is important to keep in mind that working as a team with the expert does not imply that the expert should or can testify according to the lawyer's interests if these are contrary to the truth since this is a prohibited and punishable practice.

This is why there are three situations:

→ **The first: Evaluation of the expert with the purpose of analyzing his incorporation as a party expert.**

Once we have selected the most suitable expert to carry out the task, we must review -with him/her- if the evaluation he/she will make on the expert object will bring us closer or farther away from the expected or desirable result; that is, if it will strengthen our theory of the case. After that, and only in the affirmative case, we prepare the expert points. Thirdly, he will analyze the evidentiary material or participate together with other experts in his evaluation or expertise. Finally, you will present us with your report, to which you must attach a special explanation for us, where you will explain -in concrete and simple terms- what techniques you administered, why you selected them and discarded others, and what you observed; culminating with the conclusions reached and how these relate to our position in the trial.

→ **The second: Evaluation of the expert with the purpose of incorporating him as a party expert when we do not offer points of expertise but we are going to confront (contradict) the adversary's evidence.**

This is where the expert comes as an observer of the expert's work in order to provide us with material to challenge the official report or the opposing party's report. This work must be carried out with much professionalism and seriousness, since the function is not to hinder justice, nor to delay, but to collaborate to achieve its perfection, the excellence of its resolutions. It is for this reason that I emphasize the importance of the contradictory nature of each of the evidence that will be presented in the oral trial; being the expert witness, one of them, it also corresponds here to present to the judge these two antagonistic versions that oppose and mutually control each other.

In this sense, our expert will have a different mission than the one corresponding to the first hypothesis, being then his function to attend, participate, and not consent to acts that end up contaminating the analyzed pieces of evidence, to observe traces of contamination or to alert in writing that the chain of custody has been broken. To oppose the technique used because it is outdated or because it is not the one usually applied in these cases, and also to express disagreement with the result or to leave the possibility of presenting their observations separately. It is very important, here, that the expert in any assigned task behaves as a watchman of the procedures and the results. Then, he will give us his technical report to be added to the file and, at the same time, a report to us in a more colloquial language and with special observations, which will allow us tomorrow - in the middle of the oral trial - to skillfully exercise the technique of counter-examination to the expert of the opposing party.

→ **And there is a third possibility, as important as the previous ones, which has to do with the performance of the expert simply as an advisor.**

In this case, he does not appear at the trial -at least in the first stage- but he instructs us, informs us, and provides us with information regarding the report presented by the official or opposing expert. This expert, in his role as advisor, could offer us a bibliography on the subject, expert studies, points of expertise, and material to challenge the expertise of the other party. He provides us with data on the successes and errors of the expert's material and the methods used. It gives us the basis to do our work efficiently at all stages of the process. This type of expert advisors are very useful for civil, criminal, and labor trials. I especially recommend that you incorporate trustworthy people with specific specialties in the subjects that you work on in your law firms into your staff.

The relationship between the trial lawyer and the expert witness is divided into different phases that are key to the success of the case.

Fase 1

Determinar la necesidad del perito. En esta etapa, se busca identificar si la participación de un experto es necesaria para aclarar un punto controvertido en el caso. Se evalúan las circunstancias para determinar si la experiencia y conocimientos especializados de un perito pueden brindar claridad y perspectiva.

Fase 2

Selección del perito más idóneo. Aquí se elige al perito con las mejores credenciales, ya que su testimonio será considerado una voz autorizada y no podrá ser cuestionado fácilmente por los jueces. Se busca encontrar al experto con la experiencia y el conocimiento adecuado para respaldar la posición planteada en el juicio.

Fase 3

Entrevistas previas con los peritos. Durante esta etapa, se llevan a cabo entrevistas para evaluar la idoneidad del perito y su utilidad para los objetivos propuestos. Se analiza su trayectoria, su calidad como persona y se abordan los detalles de la pericia requerida. Además, se prepara conjuntamente el testimonio para el juicio oral, utilizando herramientas de litigación oral para asegurar que su relato sea comprensible y persuasivo.

Fase 3.2

Se abordan las fortalezas y debilidades del perito, así como las posibles críticas que puedan surgir debido a su trayectoria, calidad profesional o cambios de postura. Estas cuestiones se tocan en las entrevistas previas para estar preparados y tener respuestas ensayadas ante posibles objeciones. También se discuten las debilidades del adversario y se tratan temas como las conclusiones alcanzadas, el método y los testigos utilizados.

The art of making the expert's statement understandable and, therefore, useful:

- ***Time and utility values:***

The oral nature of the proceedings, whether criminal or non-criminal, requires us to observe the values of time and utility in each action.

Being part of the system demands that we cannot delay one of the most precious values: the time of the parties involved. In this sense, we are required to be aware and responsible for all the evidence we offer and produce both in the preliminary stages and in the oral trial.

Therefore, we must refrain from presenting or requesting the performance of expert opinions that waste time or whose usefulness will not serve to clarify the facts. In line with the above, it is important that the expert understands the importance of his performance and that he commits himself to collaborating with the objectives of his presentation. If his expertise does not contribute anything, the question is why it was proposed or made.

If their expertise brings a lot to the table, but no one fully understands its usefulness, the question is why we are wasting so much potential.

Hence, our art as litigators will be to simplify the task for the court and the jurors if they are participating or if there is a possibility that they will intervene in the future oral trial. For this reason, the basis of the agreement we reach with the experts must include the need for it to be expressed in technical terms and its translation into clear and simple terms. The premise is that if we cannot understand what the expert is reporting, how can we expect an impartial third party who has no or only vague knowledge of the expertise and who does not know the facts of the case nor the positions of the parties to understand it?

The litigant, in this situation, acts as an interpreter or translator of the expert's report. He/she asks the expert as many times as necessary until he/she is able to understand in depth everything he/she has expressed.

Aspects to be addressed: The DH Method

Given that it is common for experts and those with in-depth knowledge in a given area to use technical and complex language, it is necessary for the litigant to work with the expert during the preliminary interviews on key aspects such as the expert's credibility, his or her presentation before the judge and jury, and the appropriate use of language accessible to all members of the jury, who must analyze and understand the expert's evidence. It is ideal and advisable to practice a series of open and closed questions to instruct the expert to respond in simple language during the oral trial.

It is also important to inquire here -in the previous interviews- about the method used by the expert to reach his or her conclusions, making sure that a procedure supported by the science, art, or technique in which he or she specializes has been followed. In addition to this, it is vital that the litigant understands the entire expert process in order to maintain control of his or her case for an optimal examination and, in this way, to provide convincing evidence.

Thus, it will be during the oral trial when the process followed by the expert to support his conclusions will be explained through questions.

However, it is necessary to emphasize that one should not go directly to conclusions; rather, the expert should first be prepared as an authority on the subject. Then, the method used by the expert will be addressed, and open and closed questions will be practiced to go deeper into the details.

Let us remember that litigation tools allow us to access a greater amount of information, which in turn enables us to carry out conscious and responsible work oriented to achieve the results we have proposed.

In summary, the previous work with the experts involves the following requirements:

➢ Know your personal and professional history, thus assessing your suitability to prove what the party you will represent is exposing.

➢ Know and understand his expert work on the case and how and why he came to the conclusions he did.

➢ Rehearse your cross-examination, and work on tailoring the language to the members of the courtroom; your testimony must be free of complicated jargon and technicalities. It must be understandable to all members of the court.

➢ Evaluate the weaknesses and strengths of the expert, as well as possible criticisms that may arise in this regard, and prepare to respond accordingly.

➢ Learn in detail the report generated by the expert in order to prepare a good interrogation (it is advisable to carry out evaluations and rehearsals of the questions and answers to be asked).

➢ To prepare the witnesses in order to bring in the expert witness as the expert who will give his opinion according to the optics of his knowledge, who – despite this – must be governed only by the questions asked by the litigant in order to confirm his theory of the case.

Relevance of expert evidence

As we have mentioned before, in the adversarial system, it is crucial that the evidence presented is relevant, necessary, and truly useful to elucidate the facts in question. As litigants, we have the responsibility to demonstrate this relevance.

Therefore, we cannot rely on unnecessary or superabundant evidence. It is imperative to justify the need for expert evidence or the participation of an expert to resolve the facts. This is achieved by providing direct or indirect information on the circumstances surrounding the event, which allows us to individualize the accused and give value to the victim's testimony.

The relevance of expert evidence can be analyzed from two perspectives:

- **Logical relevance:** refers to the primary and secondary facts surrounding the events. As lawyers, we must consider this level before defending the relevance of judicial evidence.

- **Legal relevance:** this is the next level to be examined. Legal relevance implies that the lawyer may offer expert evidence, but the judge must admit it as long as it does not cause prejudice. In this case, the costs and benefits of such expert evidence are evaluated. For example, in the United States, the Federal Rules of Evidence, specifically Rule 403, establishes the exclusion of expert evidence when it is not necessary or when there is a risk of confusing the jury.

It is important to understand how the law works in other countries, as this can provide insight into certain issues. During the expert investigation stage, we were able to determine whether the expert was qualified. Remember that the expert's voice will validate our theory of the case before the jury.

Experts may be recognized professionals in their fields, supported by publications, awards, or even interviews in the media. Sometimes, the expert's presence in the media indicates that they have an intellectual wealth that allows them to transmit and disseminate scientific information more easily.

These issues must be investigated. The expert's word has value, and his or her expertise in the field allows us to convey reliability to the judge and jurors.

In the case of Argentina, the National Code of Criminal Procedure establishes that it is mandatory for experts to accept the position and perform it properly. Failure to comply with this rule may result in disciplinary sanctions, such as exclusion from their registration.

This precept is one of the main distinctions between:

- ➢ an expert summoned to the trial, who has signed a report and who instructs us on a specific subject,
- ➢ and a circumstantial witness who simply witnessed an event by chance.

Optimizing the Presentation of Information at the Oral Trial

The adversarial system differs from the mixed inquisitorial system in several fundamental aspects that affect the way in which information is presented and evaluated in an oral trial.

In the adversarial system, the presentation of information before the judge requires the source to make a direct statement.

- ➔ *It requires the active participation of litigants to present and challenge evidence effectively.*
- ➔ *And it ensures that the fundamental principles of the process are respected.*

But it is often believed - erroneously - that the simple reading of an expert report submitted during the preliminary investigation stage is sufficient. It is considered that it is not necessary to summon witnesses since the report is incorporated by reading or simply requires the expert to ratify that he was the one who submitted and signed the report.

This practice violates the guarantees of the adversarial accusatory process and hinders its proper functioning, going against the principles of immediacy, contradiction, publicity, and orality.

As trial lawyers, we cannot allow an expert report to be incorporated by reading or that the expert's only function is to ratify his or her signature. We must demand that the expert be cross-examined during the oral trial hearing and provide the adversary the opportunity to cross-examine the expert. These are the bases of the adversarial accusatory system.

Necessary observations of current events in Latin American oral litigation

At the oral trial, we sometimes encounter judges who insist on retaining the power to question witnesses, and in the case of experts, they tend to jump directly to conclusions without allowing counsel to demonstrate the credibility of the expert or the method used to reach such conclusions. They then ask a few questions to supplement the information or clarify any doubts and barely give the litigants the opportunity to question the expert on these aspects.

These practices must be abandoned altogether, and as litigants, we must insist that the trial be a "trial" for us, not a "trial" for us.

Pertains to prove our theory of the case.

Cross-examination of the expert witness at the oral hearing. Steps:

During the oral argument hearing, when the litigant calls his or her expert to the stand, and the judge swears him or her in, it is common for the jury to have doubts about the expert's impartiality and loyalty to the truth. This is why exposing the expert's credibility at the outset is crucial. The attorney must demonstrate that the report is based on sound rules of the expert's area of expertise and that the conclusion reached would be the same for any other expert.

It is also essential to introduce the expert by asking open-ended questions to establish his or her identity, profession, experience, and educational background. These questions allow the judge and jury to get to know the expert in detail.

After introducing the expert, the expert must address his report, his research methodology, the formal rigor used by science in his field, and finally, the conclusions he has reached. Both the lawyer and the expert must have a deep knowledge of the subject matter under investigation to address the subject through open and closed questions, making the report clear to the members of the court.

On occasion, expert witnesses may behave in a derogatory manner towards counsel, especially if they have prior oral trial experience and feel confident to act freely. At this point, it is imperative that the attorney maintain control over the direct examination and remember that he or she is in control of the process. Although the expert is the protagonist, the lawyer must keep the reins firm through the questions, thus maintaining control over the expert.

Presentation of information. Differences between the adversarial accusatory system and the mixed inquisitorial system.

Adversarial Accusatory System	Mixed Inquisitorial System
➔ *The presentation of information at trial is based on the adversarial principle, where the parties have the opportunity to present and refute evidence orally and publicly.*	➔ *The presentation of information is more focused on the judge, who plays an active role in the investigation and collection of evidence, having greater control over the presentation of information at trial.*
➔ *The parties are responsible for presenting and arguing their own evidence, which implies that they must have full knowledge of the evidence they wish to present.*	➔ *The judge has a more active role in the collection of evidence, even being able to request and obtain evidence on his own without depending exclusively on the parties.*
➔ *Information is presented mainly through the testimony of witnesses and experts who attend the trial to be examined and cross-examined by the parties. There is an emphasis on orality and confrontation of testimony.*	➔ *The presentation of information may be more written and document-based, where the judge has a more prominent role in the assessment and analysis of the documents presented. Oral testimony may have less relevance compared to the adversarial system.*

PROFESSIONAL ADVICE

Ask yourself:

- → *Is it necessary for an expert to participate?*
- → *Which would be the most suitable?*

In addition:

- → *Do not present experts without first interviewing them.*
- → *Do not present experts because they have been recommended to you or because they are famous or well-known.*
- → *Make a list of questions that include personal issues to see if they can work in sync.*
- → *Don't let the expert take over your case.*
- → *Leads the relationship with the expert.*
- → *Make him feel part of the team.*
- → *Do not commit fraud by using the expert's report.*

CROSS-EXAMINATION OF WITNESSES

DISMANTLING THE TESTIMONY OF THE ADVERSARY WITNESS

"The lawyer doesn't go to trial to investigate the truth; he goes to prove it."

Oral Litigation Maxim 8: *"What you did not contest, refute, or prove to be untrue will be taken as truth by the judge at the time of sentencing."*

Defending the innocence of a person accused of a sexual crime can be a titanic task since, as we have been exposing, the presumption of innocence lacks relevance, and therefore, it could be said that it is mandatory for the defendants to present an alternative theory to the accusation. To be honest, it is not enough for your defendant to plead not guilty; you need to give reasons to the judge so that he considers him as such.

I will tell you the case of Marcelo, an expert and outstanding criminal lawyer whom I had the opportunity to train to face an oral trial with the aforementioned characteristics.

In that trial, he was to act as defense counsel for Rubén, a 24-year-old man accused of having committed simple sexual abuse against his 11-year-old cousin.

Marcelo, accustomed to exercising a passive defense and playing to his adversary's fault, relied during the trial and his closing argument on the principle of presumption of innocence. This led him to overlook and disregard some important variables. In other words, his strategy was to summarize everything that his adversary did not prove in order to sustain the accusation.

At present, however, this strategy is working little or not at all.

Marcelo presented very little evidence on his behalf, and the evidence he presented was not sufficiently objective to form a sufficiently strong element of conviction for the judge.

Thus, in the coaching sessions, we warned about the situation and anticipated what could happen in that trial. With the cards we had at hand, we reviewed and strengthened the strategy focused on presenting an outstanding performance in the counter examination.

We trained the technique together by establishing the issues and lines to be addressed with each of the counterpart witnesses.

Marcelo mainly focused on two or three objectives linked to questioning the existence of the fact. Thus, he was able to challenge the statement of the girl's mother when, through suggestive questions, he showed that the girl had information for adults within her reach, which contaminated all her statements.

Thanks to the early warning of these weaknesses and the inclusion in the strategy of the current problems faced by the presumption of innocence, Marcelo was able to show off in the cross-examination, presenting the judge with diverse and sustained reasons so that he could rule in Ruben's favor.

What is the importance of cross-examination in the development of the oral trial?

In the legal field, the witness occupies an essential role, being that individual who, through his senses, has been a direct participant in a specific event. It is no mere coincidence that in all nations, witnesses are invested with the inescapable obligation to communicate the truth in full compliance with the laws. Thus, the transgression of this responsibility could lead to the commission of the crime of false testimony, a constant reminder of the importance of truthfulness in the judicial process.

However, while it is premised on the assumption that witnesses appear in court with the intention of relating the facts in their entirety, this is where the fascinating concept of cross-examination comes into play. This skillful and complex method gives litigants the opportunity to orally challenge the veracity of a witness's testimony. Since this technique is one of the prerogatives attached to the adversarial system, the act of cross-examination involves inquiring into witnesses who have been previously examined by the adversary since such witnesses support the opposing party's theory of the case. In this scenario, a highly relevant consideration emerges: focusing our questions on those statements that do not favor our cause. In other words, we seek to discredit inconsistent, biased, and unreliable testimony in order to increase confidence in our own theory of the case and, at the same time, decrease confidence in the opposing position.

Key questions arise: How do you conduct effective cross-examination? Is it necessary to cross-examine each witness presented by the opposing party? How do you select which aspects to challenge in the witness statement under cross-examination?

The effectiveness of cross-examination lies in a combination of skills and strategies. The ability to formulate precise and persuasive questions is vital, as each question seeks to shed light on the veracity of the witness's statement. Careful selection of the points to probe in the witness's testimony requires a thorough understanding of one's own case and the ability to identify areas of vulnerability in the opposing testimony.

In planning and executing a successful cross-examination, it is not enough to question for the sake of questioning. Rather, it is a meticulous and strategic back-and-forth between the attorney and the witness, with the goal of uncovering the truth and putting into perspective the validity of the assertions presented.

This may help persuade the judge or jury of the validity of the position being defended.

Principles for the cross-examination of witnesses

As we have discussed in the preceding sections, the **adversarial principle is a** cornerstone of the judicial process. Its essence lies in ensuring that all parties involved in the litigation have the opportunity to question and confront every fact, evidence, question and answer presented by the other contending factions. Under this approach, each legal contender is subjected to the crucible of scrutiny, a rigorous evaluation guided by his or her adversary's theory of the case.

The **principle of equality of parties and equality of arms**, interdependent and crucial, ensures that each litigant has equal access to present their case and use the evidence they deem relevant. Cross-examination, a tool of considerable scope in the hands of the litigants, proves to be a powerful vehicle for projecting their theory of the case during the course of the trial.

In relation to the role of the judge, it is essential that he refrains from questioning witnesses during the judicial process since this could disrupt the equality of the parties, considering the authority and role he holds. Cross-examining a witness is a formidable and practically unattainable challenge for a judge since this would entail the suppression of conflicting narratives and the search for truth, which is the primary purpose of the adversarial judicial process.

In referring to the opening argument discussed in previous pages, we emphasized that the lawyer not only sets himself up as the presenter of the case but also adopts the role of a skilled salesman. This is where he cultivates the skill of selling, of persuading the judge of the strengths of his theory of the case and why the judge should consider it to be the most credible and convincing version.

Consequently, in order to consolidate a final truth, that which the judge will embrace in his ruling, it is imperative that such truth be subjected to scrutiny and critical analysis by the opposing party; the opposing counsel performs the function of communicating to the judge the imperfections, omissions, falsehoods or weaknesses in the case presented by the other side. At the same time, he must highlight the virtues of his own case while dismissing his opponent's arguments.

In this way, the fabric of the oral trial is woven. By allowing the litigants to present their arguments and debate the merits and detriments of each case, the judge will be in an optimal position to forge a fair and accurate decision.

Witness cross-examination has the potential to reshape the course of the trial – find out how to use this tool to your advantage!

Essential Tools for the Trial Lawyer in Cross-examination

Appearance	Essential Tools	Description
Investigating attorney	• *Discovery of weaknesses of the case.* • *Detailed witness analysis*	*After taking on a case, you must dive into the record, identify cracks in the opposing argument, and explore the history of witnesses to discredit their testimony.* *Leverage the use of technology to obtain detailed background information.*
Lawyer Strategist	• *Evaluation of the need for cross-examination.* • *Selection of witnesses to be counter-examined.* • *Strategy preparation.*	*You need to decide whether cross-examination is necessary, select strategic witnesses, and plan the type of attack (witness credibility or conditions of their testimony). It may include the strategic use of rival witnesses.*
Previous interview	• *Establishment of a meeting with witnesses.* • *Obtaining high-quality information.*	*It is important to interview witnesses to become familiar with their testimony and verify its authenticity. Witnesses proposed by the opposing party may be interviewed beforehand, always seeking their consent.*
Confrontation in the oral trial	• *Maintenance of control over the witness.* • *Obtaining reliable and verified information.* *Make sure to master emotions very well.*	*It resorts to the use of strategic questions. You should also make sure that the information is previously verified. Maintain control over emotions. Avoid disqualifications without irrefutable evidence and maintain a professional attitude. Use suggestive and closed questions. Adapt the thematic approach in cross-examination.*

Being a successful trial lawyer requires mastery of the art of cross-examination. Taking on a case involves transforming yourself into an insightful investigator and strategist. Below, we break down how to optimize these crucial skills:

➢ **The Investigative Attorney: The Central Skill of Cross-examination**

This is the skill that comes most alive during cross-examination. After taking on a case, either from the notitia criminis or late in the process, the first step is to dive into the file and thoroughly explore the witnesses that our adversary might present. Thus, our job as an investigator consists of the following:

- ➔ Discover the weaknesses of the case: Identify the cracks in the opposing argument.
- ➔ Analyze witnesses: Investigate the history and profile of each witness to discredit their testimony.

A meticulous investigation becomes transcendental in the process. Today's technology provides the ability to dive into the employment history, residential background, interpersonal relationships, and inner circle of witnesses. Social media platforms, for example, become a direct source of information, allowing for a thorough analysis of profiles, online connections, and even testimonies provided by other witnesses. Thoroughly exploring the scene of the crime and the site where the events took place will enrich our accumulation of data and enable us to contrast the statements made with the evidence gathered.

It is vital to investigate those who support the rival case theory. Immerse yourself in their motives and links to understand their intentions. To do this, do not hesitate to avail yourself of all the research and communication resources and facilities that today's web and globalized systems provide.

➢ The Strategic Lawyer: Planning and Cross-examination

Once the research phase is completed, planning begins. Here, the lawyer becomes a strategist.

1. Assess the need for cross-examination: After identifying weaknesses, decide whether cross-examination is appropriate.
2. Selecting witnesses for cross-examination: Not all witnesses need to be cross-examined.
3. Prepare the strategy. Evaluate the type of attack: credibility of the witness or conditions of his testimony.

Planning may include the exceptional strategy of using a rival witness to bolster your theory. It is not always impeachment; sometimes, it is reinforcement with opposing testimony.

Thus, the attorney strategist must be guided by his or her theory of the case, decide which witnesses to cross-examine, how to attack their credibility, and how to leverage their testimony to strengthen his or her position.

Ultimately, the ability to research and plan is essential in cross-examination. Becoming a skilled trial lawyer requires expertise in these fundamental tools, allowing you to challenge testimony and prove your truth in the courtroom.

➢ Previous interview

When dealing with the topic of direct examination, we emphasized the importance of the attorney establishing a meeting with the witnesses. The purpose of this practice is to become familiar with the witness's testimony and, consequently, to verify the authenticity of his or her statements. As lawyers, it is of utmost importance not to risk our credibility based on witnesses with ambiguous intentions.

In a lawyer's work environment, it is common for certain uncertainties to arise. For example, is it feasible to conduct interviews with witnesses proposed by the opposing party? The answer is absolutely yes. We can conduct interviews with witnesses in order to structure our cross-examination strategy. This approach provides us with an avenue to obtain high-quality information. Still, **it should be noted that the consent of the witness summoned by the opposing party to submit to an interview is an exception.** However, as lawyers, we should always seek to establish a channel of communication with opposing witnesses.

On many occasions, the opposing side tends to call witnesses whose contributions to its theory of the case are minimal, which can result in an attempt to address several issues in a short period of time. However, this strategy can backfire during a trial.

It is essential to remember that as trial lawyers, we have the legal prerogative to conduct preliminary interviews with witnesses in order to carefully screen and select those witnesses whose testimony strongly and consistently supports our theory of the case.

Likewise, when approaching the witness, it is essential to make our purpose clear. We must communicate that our intention is simply to ascertain information that may not be reflected in the files. The witness should always be treated courteously, acknowledging both his or her time and contribution to the case. In this context, it is essential to reiterate the importance of seeking the opportunity to interview witnesses proposed by the opposing party. The prior interview with witnesses serves a dual function: to detect vulnerabilities in the opposing party's position and to confirm the soundness of our own strategy.

Thus, we see that the trial lawyer must transcend conventional barriers; he cannot impose obstacles on himself. It is necessary to visualize opportunities beyond the obvious, always in accordance with the legal framework in force.

➢ **Seeing the witness face-to-face at the oral trial**

The fourth phase involves facing the witness during cross-examination. At this point, the witness has already been directly cross-examined by our opponent and has corroborated the facts as presented by counsel, either in the opening argument or the presentation of evidence.

Once our adversary completes his cross-examination, we assume the floor. This is where a number of guidelines become essential for every trial lawyer:

➢ **Recommendation 1: Maintain control over the witness**

To do this effectively, we must employ strategic questions that lead to the previously established objectives. This approach may include attacking the internal and external perception of the witness, as well as his or her credibility, by using leading questions – in cross-examination, we rely on leading questions – those that implicitly contain the answer. While these questions are not appropriate for direct examination, they are legitimate during cross-examination.

Clarification: Although procedural rules may limit the use of leading questions during cross-examination, we must defend their usefulness, as they allow us to sift through witness statements and present an alternative perspective to the judge and jury.

To clarify, leading questions are those that admit only yes or no answers to facts that are irrefutable to the witness. The proper method of cross-examination involves asking leading questions one at a time, starting with those that the witness cannot deny, before surprising with a shocking question.

It is not appropriate for counsel to conclude with the witness; the ruling or conclusion should be reserved until the closing argument. It is at that time that we will present it, strengthening our theory of the case. We do not seek the opinion of the witness. The opinion is ours, and we present it in our closing argument.

▫ *Clarification: When we conduct the direct examination with our witness, it is advisable to do so chronologically so that the judge and jury understand the sequence of events. However, in cross-examination, we opt for a thematic approach, addressing issues from minor to major, always seeking surprise as a key element. To achieve this, we manipulate the pace of the statement, starting calmly and gradually building up to the surprise factor.*

➢ **Recommendation 2: Obtain reliable and verified information beforehand.**

The basis of this process lies in ensuring the effectiveness of this phase and maintaining absolute control over the cross-examination.

➢ **Recommendation 3: Preserving the trial lawyer's emotional control**

The intense adrenaline rush experienced at trial demands that our strategy be grounded in solid planning and in perfect alignment with our theory of the case.

It is crucial to remember that we are facing a witness whose mission is to discredit our theory of the case, which is in direct contradiction with our objectives. Therefore, it is of utmost importance to retain control and ensure the subsistence of our goals.

Thus, it is vital for the lawyer to maintain his or her emotional balance and to anticipate any contingencies that may arise during the trial. By anticipating, we gain clarity and can foresee and manage the motions more effectively.

Following our plan ensures the continuation of the credibility we gained by presenting our opening argument.

Here, I must emphasize that emotional control is achieved by sticking to our plan and maintaining a professional and credible attitude, which are elements that constitute our most powerful cover letter. In this same context, adopting a hostile attitude towards the witness is counterproductive; it is more effective to demonstrate through cross-examination that the witness has made a mistake.

Branding a witness as a liar should be avoided unless there is irrefutable evidence to support a manifest corruption of intent. In the case of confronting a hostile witness, one who persists in his assertions despite distorting the truth or having a limited understanding of the facts, we have an arsenal of cross-examination tools: repeat the same question in different ways three times; address the witness with honorific treatment (such as "esteemed," "graduate," "sir"); start with facts that the witness cannot deny.

In this regard, it is important to point out that, although we use leading questions at this stage, it is advisable to introduce the witness directly at the beginning of the cross-examination, thus encouraging a fluid dialogue.

As the cross-examination progresses, we can use closed questions, which address specific issues, although we must remember that their use is limited, as our standard is the leading question.

However, the use of open-ended questions is not recommended, as we do not intend for the witness to develop his or her testimony at this stage. Our intention is to validate our theory of the case over that of our adversary, and the most effective way to do this is through direct questions that give us mastery of the narrative.

In short, cross-examination, that lucid and powerful tool in the litigator's arsenal, transcends the simple confrontation of witnesses. It stands as a key piece in the construction of solid arguments and in the constant search for the truth in the judicial process. Its mastery requires not only technical skill but also the acumen to identify opportunities that can challenge the opposing party's narrative and consolidate the strength of one's own case. It exemplifies the intricate activity that underlies the judicial process, where skill and strategy intertwine to reveal the truth that lies beneath the surface of testimony.

PROFESSIONAL ADVICE

- ★ *Prepare yourself very well for the counter examination by means of exercises.*
- ★ *When performing this technique, remember your theory of the case and stick to your plan.*
- ★ *You should not ask too many questions.*
- ★ *Leave the conclusion to the closing argument.*
- ★ *Keep control of your emotions; don't get carried away by the moment.*
- ★ *Treat the witness well.*
- ★ *Remember that the goal is to persuade by telling a story (the lawyer's "storytelling" skill).*

HOW TO CROSS-EXAMINE AN EXPERT?

MASTERING THE ART OF CHALLENGING THE EXPERTS AND OVERTURNING THE STRENGTH OF THE EXPERT REPORT

When it comes to the dispute to be resolved in court, experts and experts emerge as key players, possessing specialized knowledge in crucial areas who, having previously prepared reports during the investigation stage, are called to the oral trial by the parties involved to shed light on their findings. Beyond their simple participation, the presence and competence of these experts prove to be fundamental elements in the balance of truth and justice.

In this sense, it is useful to share a maxim of Eastern philosophy expressed by the great master **Lao Tse,** which I consider applicable to the art of oral litigation, which teaches us that: ***"He who dominates others is strong, he who dominates himself is powerful."***

I thought it appropriate to quote this phrase because it explains very well the temperament we should adopt when we have to deal with difficult witnesses, as is often the case when we cross-examine experts.

During the trial, we go through highly stressful situations, such as when the expert witness expresses himself using concepts that are totally foreign to our specialty, refers to procedures that we have never performed or know how to perform, or gives us confusing explanations.

Some experts, when summoned to testify in court, for whatever reason, do not want to defend their position, even when they have investigated and signed their report. They usually express themselves in a technical and ambiguous way, as if they wanted to tell us that it could be this way or that way.

You have to be very prepared to control your temperament and apply the technique in spite of these variables.

There are also those who are reluctant to provide explanations because they want to maintain a certain degree of secrecy.

Not to mention those who do not answer our suggestive questions, and who talk too much and utter empty words. Or worse, those who present us with an unfriendly or even hostile attitude.

It is under these circumstances that we must raise our tolerance levels and, of course, control our temperament so as not to incur an attitude that could ruin everything we have achieved.

Therefore, each question we ask must make sense; it must be the result of everything we have investigated. Each question must demonstrate that we are not interested in competing with the expert but only in collaborating so that the judge can access the truth.

This brief summary of the complex situations that arise in the trial brings to mind the time when I witnessed a very particular civil trial in the United States. The issue was to establish whether a former partner of an important company was entitled to obtain the million-dollar indemnity she was claiming for her withdrawal from the company.

The former partner also alleged that she was suffering from certain physical and mental health disorders caused by the abuse committed by her partners.

In addition to the fact that we heard several expert witnesses, including doctors, psychologists, etc., I would like to focus on the participation of an expert in accounting with several master's degrees in business.

The expert witness, whom we will call Phillip, took the stand and swore to tell the truth. The plaintiff's counsel began his extensive repertoire of open-ended questions, which took approximately 2 hours.

Everything was so organized that the expert responded to the questions posed by the litigant by exhibiting documents in which he had dumped his research. First, he took some balance sheets out of his briefcase, and later, he asked for some graphs to be shared on the screens. To close, he took a kind of rigid cardboard about 2 meters long, which he asked to be hung on a blackboard and then used to continue his complete and complex exposition.

All of us present were perplexed by such preparation. The expert witness said that it reflected the fluctuations in the company's income and the percentages that the plaintiff was entitled to receive. It was truly a display worthy of admiration.

But the most exciting thing happened when it was the defendant's lawyer's turn. A somewhat rudimentary lawyer, anxious to get started, he was nevertheless very cordial the whole time.

He did not use reports, nor did he display graphics or spend large sums of money to display those rigid posters.

He made use of all the supports that his adversary had used. From the corporal, the lawyer appeared confident but somewhat impatient, and given the small size of the courtroom, when his opponent objected, he smiled at him and touched his shoulders. So much physical contact with his opponent really surprised me.

Step by step, the litigant was getting to the point at issue. He did not have many issues to attack, and his lines of cross-examination at first seemed somewhat imprecise.

The magic happened when, for example, he asked the expert in calculations and numbers to answer whether he had contemplated in his extensive research how much the company had spent on medical treatment to support the plaintiff's mental health. To which the expert responded in the affirmative. He then asked if this was reflected in any of the documents exhibited.

The surveyor nodded. Later, the lawyer asked Phillip to show his reports again and asked him to go page by page looking for the information, which, to everyone's surprise, was not found to be overturned.

He asked to show the magistrate those charts, where it said medical expenses, and asked, "Did you include there the therapies and medicines that the company paid for?"

To which he replied, "Yes, I did dump all the information they had provided me."

The lawyer returned to the same point and asked: "Who provided who?"

"Mrs. Stefani."

The litigant felt he was getting to the point:

"Did you not ask the Respondent to show you all the expenses? He replied that no, it was not necessary."

"You also did not go to the company to extract the information to make your reports?"

"No, I called twice, but nobody answered."

"Did you also not submit a formal request for access to such documents?"

"No, that is taken care of by the lawyer."

"We can, therefore, say that the information you displayed in graphs, reports, and banners is incomplete."

... did not allow the expert to respond and stated, "I have no further questions for the "expert"."

And he reserved what that meant for his closing argument. As you can see, good self-management and self-control allowed the anxious but prepared litigator to dominate the situation and get the point he had gone after.

General guidelines:

In this sense, we must be very clear that it is not a matter of counter-examining the expert to show that what he did is wrong because there you will only find resistance. It is a matter of helping him to express with the necessary words that perhaps there are details that he missed, he did not follow the procedure, and the reliability of the result lacks confrontation and, therefore, support.

First, it is essential for us, the litigants, to establish the expert's relevance to the case, ensuring that his or her presence is crucial to clarify the matter in question. Secondly, we must demonstrate the expert's competence by highlighting his or her track record, recognition, and credentials, as well as the endorsement of other specialists in his or her field.

These aspects will support the use of the expert report provided by the expert. Now, the question arises: Is it necessary to cross-examine each expert witness? The art of cross-examining experts is a skill that requires time and practice to perfect due to its high degree of complexity. However, the act of cross-examination reaches an even higher level of intricacy. Thus, we enter a realm where the fundamental question is: how to identify the fissures in the report presented by the expert? How to ensure that the expert report that the litigant has presented prevails?

Before the oral battle begins, the trial lawyer must embrace his or her role as a strategist with commitment and mastery. Preparation is key, and to diligently fulfill this mission, the attorney must remember the four preceding phases.

In order to exercise our work with the utmost professional zeal, it is essential to internalize the four preliminary phases that every trial lawyer must approach with mastery and success.

Phase 1: Research

This preliminary stage will be addressed through a set of specific objectives.

→ Objective 1

Get to know the surveyor; inquire into the person behind the role he or she has assumed. It is imperative to understand broad aspects of his or her life, from residence and employment to personal interests, social connections, and affiliations. We seek to discern their particular inclinations regarding the matter and whether their ideological stance might impact the case at hand.

In addition, it is essential to determine whether he already had any ties with the parties involved prior to the trial and what his relationship is with the litigant who has appointed him.

→ Objective 2

To trace the expert's educational background, professional experience, and expertise in a specific discipline. This purpose leads us to explore his or her academic background, investigate whether he or she has published works or presented theses, and delve into his or her curriculum vitae. In addition, we will analyze his reputation and how he is perceived by his colleagues in his role as an expert.

From this inquiry, we can identify possible ideological tendencies and biases that the opposing expert might harbor, which could influence his or her conclusions. It is also crucial to unravel the underlying motive for the results he presents in his reports, especially if his analysis varies significantly in a particular case despite sharing the same factual basis.

It is essential to emphasize that, in the adversarial system, the expert does not hold an official position and is, therefore, not subordinate to the judge. Consequently, it is the parties who select and propose the expert to contribute his or her perspective to the theory of the case in question.

Phase 2: Planning

At this stage, we will deploy our skills as strategists, carefully assessing the appropriateness of conducting the cross-examination of an expert witness. It is crucial to keep in mind that the expert witness is the expert in the matter, not us, so we will avoid engaging in fruitless role-playing. The decision to cross-examine the expert must be based on solid reasons supported by evidence, with the objective of questioning the credibility of the expert and the conclusions reached.

In this phase, we will have to determine the following aspects:

- *Perform the counter-examination of the expert?*
- *What aspects should we focus on during the process?*
- *Is it advisable to collaborate with an expert advisor, such as an expert witness or specialist, to obtain comprehensive guidance on the report submitted by the opposing party's expert?*

It is highly advisable to consider the collaboration of a party advisor at this stage, either in conjunction with your own expert or with another expert in the field. This advice will be invaluable for gathering information, reviewing the bibliography, and collecting materials that will enhance our strategy in the oral trial. Additionally, this collaboration will allow us to fine-tune our cross-examination, making sure to ask pertinent questions.

Careful planning and strategic collaboration are essential at this stage to ensure that our argument at trial is effective and persuasive. Careful selection of the issues to be addressed and a focus on refuting the credibility of the opposing expert will enable us to build a strong and convincing defense.

Phase 3: Pre-interview

First of all, the possibility of conducting a preliminary interview with the opposing party's expert is largely limited since such occasions rarely materialize due to the possible partiality of the parties or the tight schedule of the expert.

Despite this eventuality, this preliminary inquiry stage can be effectively replaced by a thorough analysis of the reports documented in the file. We refer to the previous statements made by the expert in the framework of the presentation of evidence.

Now, the first step is to immerse ourselves in the exhaustive study of the statements made by the expert in the reports submitted. These must be within our reach, ready to be examined at trial in case contradictions, ambiguities or statements that require further clarification arise.

To enrich this information, we will also seek to trace possible interviews that the expert witness may have given to the media, where available. This will allow us to establish links between his position expressed at trial and his public comments, adding a deeper level of understanding.

Phase 4: Oral Trial

At this culminating stage, the lawyer enters the role of litigator, where preparation and mastery of knowledge and technique are essential to confront an expert witness. Therefore, the cross-examination must reach a level of excellence supported by a deep intellectual level.

One strategic tactic for trial counsel might be to argue that the case does not require an expert witness or expert, arguing that his or her intervention does not provide clarity and that the matter could be resolved by appealing to the judge's or jury's expertise based on experience.

Second, there is the need to undermine the credibility of the expert by questioning his or her identity beyond the professional setting, challenging him or her based on the findings of phase 1. By exploring his background, the judge and jury can be persuaded of the expert's lack of integrity, exposing the interference of personal interests and clouded objectivity.

Lines of argumentation:

- *Tarnished reputation*
- *Personal prejudices*
- *Interests at stake*
- *Limited experience*
- *Lack of expertise in the subject matter in question*
- *Doubtful accreditations*

When approaching the crime scene, it is essential to investigate whether the evidence has been handled according to the correct protocols and whether the chain of custody has been preserved. In addition, it must be verified whether the laboratory used to analyze the evidence is properly accredited. The variables are diverse, which requires the litigator to be alert to identify and analyze such nuances.

→ *Procedure*

That said, as trial lawyers, it is crucial to verify that the expert has used appropriate methods and procedures, standardized or accepted by the scientific community or the community to which the expert belongs. In this way, it is also crucial to inquire whether the expert has acted in an experimental context. These are details that trial counsel can (and should) explore and challenge through cross-examination.

☞ Thirdly, the expert presents his conclusions. At this point, our task is to question whether his conclusion is the only possible one. Are they certainties or mere probabilities? Let us remember that you cannot convict someone based solely on assumptions.

At this stage, we can also question and contrast our expert's conclusions with those of the opposing expert. Based on phase 3, we will have the tools to refute the theory presented by the opposing expert.

Sometimes, in an oral trial, it happens that the experts on both sides may have good reputations and credibility, which may leave the judge at a crossroads. In this context, the litigator must exercise his role diligently during cross-examination, persuading the judge to give weight to our expert's conclusions rather than those of the adversary.

It is essential to destabilize the opposing party's theory of the case, including subjecting it to scrutiny by questioning experts in the field.

Cross-examination of the expert: mastering the technique of cross-examination

From the outset, the strategy in which we must immerse ourselves in questioning the expert is based on the art of leading questions, those that contain the answer that can only be affirmed with a yes or denied with a no.

Our approach is to approach point by point, starting with questions to which the expert is obliged to answer with a yes. This approach seeks to dismantle the initial resistance that the expert may present, as it is natural that his or her first reaction will be one of caution. After overcoming this threshold, we move thematically towards weaknesses, exploring their background, reputation, report, and ideology, among other aspects.

The strategy is to ask questions that focus on a single point, one fact at a time. This precise approach allows us, subsequently, to delve into questions that expose the expert's lack of credibility. Our purpose is to erode that initial strength that the expert may present and, consequently, to undermine the opposing party's theory.

Maintaining control in cross-examination

Cross-examining an expert witness is a challenging task; how do we manage to maintain control over an expert on the stand?

In the first instance, **it is imperative that we always keep our theory of the case in mind.** This approach provides us with a solid guide to conducting cross-examination more effectively. We must not allow ourselves to fall into the game that the expert may propose; the control rests in the hands of the attorney. If the expert attempts to expand his answers, it is our task to limit his scope. We prevent his answers from going beyond yes or no; this is why asking open-ended questions carries significant risk.

In view of this, and knowing that in the essence of our role as trial lawyers lies the importance of being honorable individuals, regardless of the adversary we face, it is essential to treat the expert witness with the utmost respect and without hostility. In other words, we value their contributions, but we also allow the judge to discern the truth through our performance.

In short, we recognize that cross-examination of the expert is a tricky technique that requires thorough preparation. To this end, it is essential to acquire detailed information and carefully select the questions to be asked at trial. Thorough preparation is key to successfully developing this challenging technique.

Our ability to navigate these tumultuous waters of information and testimony can make all the difference in the resolution of our case. By following these principles and honing our skills, we will be better equipped to face and master the cross-examination of the expert witness at trial.

Mastering the technique of cross-examination of experts:

Interrogation technique	➔ *It is based on suggestive questions that can be answered with a yes or no answer. The initial focus is to obtain affirmative answers.* ➔ *Precise point-by-point questions seek to overcome the expert's initial resistance.* ➔ *The strategy advances thematically towards the expert's weaknesses, exploring various aspects such as his background and ideology.*
Maintaining control in cross-examination	➔ *Keep in mind the theory of the case to guide cross-examination.* ➔ *Prevent the expert from expanding his answers beyond yes or no, limiting their scope.* ➔ *The importance of treating the expert with respect and without hostility, valuing his or her contributions is emphasized.* ➔ *The control of the cross-examination lies with the lawyer, and one must avoid falling into the game proposed by the expert.*
Thorough preparation	➔ *Recognize that cross-examination is a delicate technique that requires careful preparation.* ➔ *Acquire detailed information and carefully select questions to present at trial.*

PROFESSIONAL ADVICE

★ *"Use the expert to defeat the expert and you will be victorious."*

DH

THE THEORY OF OBJECTIONS

Swift as the wind, swift and devastating as fire, so must the litigant act when objecting"

DH.

Roxana, a fierce litigator, was feared and loved. One of those lawyers who leave traces in her wake. No one, absolutely no one wanted a case in which Roxana was their rival. But Fernando had no other choice.

Roxana knew what she was causing in others, and this gave her a certain enjoyment and greater security. She was convinced that Fernando would not be a threat.

Fernando, on the other hand, had a low profile and experience in the field, but no major victories were known on his part.

Until the day finally came when both had to face each other in that case where a crime of threats was being investigated.

The presiding judge opened the trial, and both litigants presented their opening arguments. Roxana showed off her oratory skills, and her eloquence left everyone in the courtroom in awe.

Fernando, on the other hand, seemed to be somewhat insecure; his erroneous attitude in his pleadings made him think that Roxana had the case won.

Then, the way was opened for the witnesses. The first to question was Fernando. Roxana had everything ready; she knew her objection lines by heart. She was known in court as the queen of objections. She knew the whole catalog perfectly.

At the beginning, Fernando found it somewhat complicated, and his trembling voice made it difficult to understand the content and meaning of his questions. Thus, the judge repeatedly called his attention to him.

Roxana was anxiously waiting for the right moment to catch her rival. However, he was only able to raise a few weak objections, which the judge overruled, and

Fernando continued to do his job. As he asked questions and the answers were granted, he built up a story that found no valid interruptions from Roxana.

But what had happened? What was wrong with Roxana? Why were the objections of no use to her this time?

The answer is simple: Diego had studied both his case and his rival; he knew that he should not give her a chance and that any wrongly formulated question could give Roxana room to act. He did not want it to come to that. So he planned every question, rehearsed to exhaustion, and finally disarmed the play of who, supported by his reputation, stopped updating and training with this kind of silent enemies.

In short, it is important to do a good job of interrogating to eliminate these interruptions. Just as important is the knowledge that your objections will not hurt your opponent if they are not backed up by building a strong case expressed through a powerful narrative.

Objections, in the legal field, refer to the reasons or arguments presented by a party for the purpose of challenging an idea or proposal put forward by the opposing party in order to avoid its acceptance or implementation. The notion of objection is fundamental in the context of oral litigation strategies and is used so that the litigant can exercise direct control over all the information that enters the process. In other words, it provides us with a method of supervision in relation to the activity being carried out by my opponent.

Their role goes beyond pointing out differences of opinion; in fact, they reveal themselves as a fundamental strategic resource that shapes and guides the dynamics of the judicial process. This strategic approach contributes to the careful filtering of relevant information while structuring and guiding the development of the litigation, with the ultimate goal of ensuring success in the dispute at hand.

Litigants may object to our adversary for different reasons. It may be to prevent him from entering irrelevant, repetitive, or prejudicial information, among others. The truth is that it is very common to act impulsively when objecting, like someone who slips out a swear word or slaps a hand when he is in a threatening or stressful situation. Many times, we object because we want to get out of a mess, and for that reason, interrupting the colleague's performance seems to give us a good alternative.

In these situations, we object not because there is something wrong or irregular but because it is our impulsive way of reacting in the midst of a rapidly unfolding trial. So, we are not objecting to the question since there is no real cause to do so, but objecting to put sticks in our opponent's wheel.

Like any impulsive act, it is thoughtless; we go from act to action without being able to measure the consequences.

Acting in a heated manner often makes us look sloppy, unprofessional, and also insecure or, even worse, fearful of the information we are trying to introduce.

Regardless of whether the judge resolves the issue, whether for or against the objection if we use this valuable resource repeatedly and without basis, the judge will think, let alone the members of the jury, that you are afraid of something or that there is certain information that you are trying to hide.

So let's see below how effective preparation of your case, knowledge of strengths and weaknesses, and how proper research can save you from these blunders that many make and can't avoid.

The strategic importance of the objection in relation to the theory of the case.

It is essential to have a clear notion of the phase of the oral trial in which we find ourselves. The judicial process begins with the opening argument, in which the litigants establish their position before the judge and jury. This is followed by the examination and cross-examination of witnesses. As opposing counsel plays his or her role, it is imperative that we pay active attention to their statements in order to discern any deviation from the theory of the case set forth in the opening argument.

Sitting at his desk, the lawyer exercises control over the information that is introduced in the trial. In this context, the tool of objection arises, which is used to ensure that the information admitted meets the following criteria:

- ➢ *Legality: The information does not refer to evidence that was previously excluded in earlier phases of the process.*
- ➢ *Relevance: The information aligns with the strategy outlined in the litigant's theory of the case.*
- ➢ *Respect for the constitutional rights and guarantees of the party it represents without violating procedural regulations.*

Throughout the oral trial, the judge will be attentive to the various objections raised and the issues they may raise. The objection becomes a vital resource to maintain consistency between the theory of the case and the evidence presented, thus ensuring a fair and equitable trial.

Cross-examination and objections at trial

In the process of cross-examining witnesses at trial, various situations can arise, and these can be divided into two key scenarios. If the attorney has conducted prior interviews with the witnesses, he or she will have an advantage in maintaining solid control over the cross-examination. However, in the absence of such preparation, there is a possibility that control will be lost, which in turn will alert the opposing party to closely monitor his opponent's actions.

In this context, the lawyer not only handles the information he introduces in the trial but also the professional performance of his colleague. Objections arise as an avenue of protest that shapes an oral advocacy. Crucially, we must object immediately when an inappropriate question is asked. The acuity of our senses will be critical in recording the other lawyer's statements verbatim and verifying whether they are in line with his or her strategy.

Precision at the time of objecting is essential; otherwise, the opportunity will be lost. Once the witness has answered the question that we consider inappropriate, the objection becomes ineffective. In parallel, the judge must make a decision at the same instant the objection is made to ensure the continuity of the oral trial.

Mastering both the art of cross-examination and the strategic handling of objections is critical to a successful attorney in court. These elements not only influence the presentation of evidence but also the pace and direction of the trial. Being prepared and agile in the use of objections can be a decisive factor in the pursuit of justice and the achievement of our client's goals.

Relevance of objections in litigation

Objections in the legal process play a fundamental role in the defense of our interests. They serve multiple purposes, all aimed at safeguarding the foundations of our legal strategy and ensuring a fair and equitable procedure.

- First, objections are a valuable tool for safeguarding the integrity of our theory of the case. By timely and accurately challenging certain elements presented by the opposing party, we ensure that the version we support at trial remains coherent and solid.
- In addition, objections allow us to exercise effective control over our adversary's theory of the case. By objecting to elements that may weaken our position and favor his, we build a defensive barrier that prevents counterproductive arguments from taking center stage in court.
- These legal interventions also serve to protect the constitutional and procedural rights of the party we represent. By objecting to evidence or arguments that may infringe on these fundamental rights, we ensure a fair and equitable legal process for all parties involved.

- Crucially, objections are essential to maintaining the adversarial principle at trial. By pointing out discrepancies, inaccuracies, or possible distortions in the testimony and evidence presented, we promote a transparent and thorough debate where each side has the opportunity to refute and counter the assertions of the other.
- Finally, objections generate strategic reservations for later stages, such as appeals. When an objection is not admitted by the court, it is crucial to record our disagreement and the reasons behind it. This lays the groundwork for a possible appeal to higher instances and ensures that procedural errors do not go unchallenged.

Methodology of objection in the judicial process

The objection technique stands as a simple and effective tool in the legal environment, where it is sufficient for the litigant to audibly exclaim "objection," followed by the reason, e.g., "suggestive objection." This ensures that the filing of the objection is duly recorded in the file.

Under this circumstance, the judge assumes different roles to resolve the situation. If the question asked is suggestive, redundant, or confusing, the judge will hear the objection and ask the litigant to reformulate his or her questioning. However, if the challenged question deals with prohibited matters, opinions, or evidence based on hearsay, the judge will deny rephrasing, as these matters are inadmissible in adversarial proceedings. This rule applies to both parties in litigation, which emphasizes the need to avoid this type of questions so as not to waste the opportunity to prove the facts we wish to support.

Once opposing counsel has restructured the challenged question, it is imperative to remain vigilant to prevent the reintroduction of information prohibited by other means. If the judge sustains the objection and the attorney correctly rephrases his question, the witness will proceed to answer. However, if the judge overrules the objection, the interrogator will lose a valuable resource and must find a legitimate and effective way to accomplish his or her purpose.

In the procedural scenario, we find one party seeking to introduce information while the opposing party opposes on the basis of its objectives. The judge, impartial, acts as the arbiter of this contest.

The judge may both admit the objection and probe the objecting attorney for further details beyond the pithy "suggestive objection" justification. This is particularly evident in the face of irrelevant or confusing questions. The judge may also give the interrogating attorney the opportunity to defend his or her position in relation to the objection raised.

The premise of equality of parties, fundamental in the judicial system, is reflected in this dynamic, where both parties find in the objection a tool to ensure that the evidence presented adheres to the established standards and meets the objective of achieving fair and equitable litigation.

Equality of parties in the **adversarial** process

The rationale for the adversarial process lies in ensuring equality of parties and fairness in the legal contest. In this context, the judge plays a crucial role in overseeing and balancing the interests of both parties to ensure a fair and equitable process.

However, what happens when the judge himself raises an objection to a question? The rules of oral litigation provide that the judge may do so exceptionally. This situation arises, for example, when a possible violation of constitutional rights, such as the right against self-incrimination, is detected.

Likewise, the judge may intervene if he perceives that the accused is in a defenseless position, even if he has a lawyer. In such cases, the judge will interpose an objection to readjust the litigants' strategies. Let us remember that the judge acts as the director of the process and is obliged to preserve the constitutional guarantees in each particular situation.

Essential requirements for effective objection

The ability to object in court is a vital tool for any trial lawyer. However, in order for an objection to be successful and not end up hurting us, it is essential to keep in mind certain crucial requirements.

- Timeliness: Timeliness is key when objecting. It should be made before the witness responds or the litigant finishes the question. Sometimes, the speed of the witness can make a late objection improper. In situations where the judge does not hear our objection, we should raise the grounds for a later appeal.
- Accuracy: Accuracy is essential in the basis of the objection. It must fit the specific situation of the trial. Each objection must be supported by a strong argument that fits the theory of the case.
- Strategy: The objection must be strategic, not merely an interruption. Its use must be aligned with the overall strategy of the case. Each step in the trial, including objections, must be congruent with the previously outlined theory of the case.

It is critical to object when the theory of the case is undermined, and we have a strong foundation. If the opposing litigant is doing his or her job and does not affect our theory, objecting may be counterproductive. The choice to object must be careful and supported by sound strategy.

Important considerations

When faced with a popular jury, the objection becomes even more relevant. In contrast to a court of experienced judges, poorly stated objections can confuse the jury, doing more harm than good.

If the colleague asks an argumentative question that introduces information through our testimony instead of the witness, the objection may not be sufficient to clarify the situation. In this context of rapid factual succession, an ineffective objection could damage our reputation.

Objecting is an art that requires care, caution, and foresight. Its execution must be commensurate with the situation and in line with the overall strategy of the case. Ultimately, a successful objection can contribute significantly to building a strong and persuasive case in court.

Types of objections in oral proceedings

Within the framework of the oral trial, we encounter various categories of objections, some of which are established by procedural rules, while others emerge from common practice.

The Anglo-Saxon legal system provides us with a wide range of objections, taking advantage of the general rules of evidence that govern the evidentiary field as a whole. This panorama presents us with a wide variety of possibilities, with more than twenty types of objections available for application. In this context, we will focus our attention on the most relevant and recurrent in the context of the oral trial.

Among the most common objections is the objection of leading questions during direct examination. At this stage, the witness takes the lead role, and the attorney should not ask leading questions that distort the witness' role. Before the witness responds with a "yes" or "no" answer, it is appropriate to use the "Leading Question" objection. However, there are two notable exceptions. First, when the question does not address a controversial point (e.g., "Are you a cousin of the defendant?"). Second, when we face a hostile witness during direct examination; the rules permit leading questions in this circumstance.

Leading or bad faith questions, posed with dishonest intentions to mislead or deceive the witness, are totally forbidden. During the trial, only the presentation of substantive information is allowed, excluding any trickery incompatible with procedural rules and litigation principles. Consequently, this type of questioning is prohibited both in direct and cross-examination.

On the other hand, ambiguous, vague, or confusing questions that lack clarity as to the attorney's intent are equally problematic. Precision is crucial in questioning to ensure adequate responses from the witness. Thus, questions must be formulated with sufficient specificity to elicit the necessary information.

We can also find the impertinent question, which arises when it is not related to the disputed facts or the positions of the parties. The opening argument establishes the relevance of the evidence presented. Often, litigants employ impertinent questions to divert attention and divert the course of the trial. In these situations, it is our duty to object with an "objection, impertinent" so that the question is properly tailored.

During the oral trial, we seek to elicit information that the witness often does not want to provide. On cross-examination, we may ask reiterative or repeated questions to emphasize an answer, but on direct examination, repeating a question after it has been answered is not appropriate and may be objected to with an "objection, reiterative."

An interesting objection relates to questions that misrepresent the evidence, i.e., those that attempt to change the evidence or introduce information that has not been previously presented. These questions should be objected to. For example, if a witness testified to having seen one of the parties with a knife, asking, "What size was the knife?" attempts to introduce information that the witness did not initially provide, which is against the rules of cross-examination.

Often, these questions are not malicious on the part of the attorney but the result of a confusion between the information gathered during the investigation and that presented at trial. The attorney may know that the defendant had a knife, in this case, a knife, but during cross-examination, he forgets the necessary intellectual steps and asks a question that misrepresents the information.

Compound questions are those that address multiple facts at once, making it difficult for the witness to answer. For example, asking, "Were you at the restaurant with your wife the night the police were looking for John for robbery?" introduces too much information at once. In this case, we should object and ask the judge to rephrase the question to address each fact separately.

Often, journalists use this approach to argue while asking questions in interviews, but in the oral trial, it is not allowed. It is crucial to ask specific questions to support our theory of the case.

Speculative questions invite the witness to make value judgments or hypotheses rather than establish concrete facts. At trial, we look for clear facts rather than speculation. For example, asking, "Do you think Francisco believed the document was legitimate when he signed it?" is not appropriate since the witness is not an expert witness and cannot determine the legitimacy of the document or know Francisco's thoughts at the time.

Instead of speculative questions, we should focus on verifiable facts and avoid value judgments or assumptions in the testimony.

In the art of cross-examination, it is essential to avoid argumentative questions. For these questions give the question itself a qualification, meaning, and relevance that should be reserved for the closing argument. For example, asking, "From where you were standing, there was no way for you to see the victim being beaten," is argumentative. At oral argument, counsel should establish the factual basis and may ask about details such as distance or the brightness of the scene but should not draw conclusions that call into question the credibility of the witness.

Another important objection relates to preventing indirect information. At trial, witnesses must relate what they perceived with their own senses, so references to what others saw or heard are prohibited, as they limit the opportunity for contradiction. A witness may not talk about what others told him or her or rely on hearsay. For example, if a lawyer asks, "What is the opinion of the neighbors about Maximiliano Perez?" we must object, as this is reference evidence, something prohibited in an oral trial.

One objection that becomes clearer with the litigator's experience is related to questions about privileged or reserved matters. This involves kinship relationships, professional relationships, religious beliefs, and more. Privileged matter encompasses information a lawyer has about his or her clients that must be kept confidential. This also applies to confessions made in religious contexts. The law seeks to protect these relationships from arbitrary interference, preserving confidentiality and respect for certain spheres of privacy.

Objecting to questions about the character of a person, whether the defendant or the victim, is essential in a trial. Sometimes, we try to prove a fact based on assumptions, which is prohibited in criminal law. The focus must be on the act under investigation, not what someone may have done before.

Another reason to object to these questions is their ability to distort perception, especially that of the jury. This is especially true when it comes to the character of the victim. For example, in a sexual abuse case, if the attorney attempts to minimize harm by questioning the victim's morality, these questions should be rejected outright.

Types of objections in oral proceedings

Type of objection	*Description*
Suggestive question	*Objecting when questions distort the role of the witness, especially in direct examination.*
Trick question	*Objecting to dishonest questions that mislead or deceive the witness.*

Ambiguous question	*Objecting to questions that lack clarity in the attorney's intent.*
Impertinent question	*Objecting to questions unrelated to the disputed facts.*
Misrepresenting question the test	*Objecting when questions attempt to change the evidence presented.*
Compound question	*Objecting to questions that address multiple facts at once.*
Speculative question	*Objecting to questions that invite the witness to make value judgments or hypotheses.*

Objection to a response

During cross-examination, it is critical to ensure that the witness's answers are clear, relevant, and free of conjecture. Here are some key objections:

Objection to non-response: if the witness refuses to answer a question or begins to ramble on about topics not asked, you should object. We are looking for specific information that the witness does not provide.

Objection to conclusions of the witness: when the witness makes conjectures or gives technical opinions for which he or she is not qualified, this is objectionable. Conclusions must be based on facts, not assumptions.

The purpose of these objections is to ensure that the information presented at trial is accurate and relevant and does not lead to confusion or erroneous conclusions by the court. Our goal is to protect the integrity of the decisions that the judge may make.

Objection in opening and closing arguments

During the opening argument, litigants present their case as if they are selling their theory of the case. This speech sets the stage for the trial by stating their position on the facts and evidence they will present. However, it is crucial to remember that no argument can be made at this point, as the facts are matters of evidence.

Nor may one argue about the evidence or its credibility. If an attorney mentions evidence in his opening argument, he should not argue about it. Evidence should be presented and discussed during cross-examination, not in the opening argument.

This also applies when a prosecutor mentions prior arrangements or agreements with the defendant that were not concluded. He cannot argue about these matters or make value judgments, as this would taint the information and violate the presumption of innocence. Guilt must be determined at the oral trial, and anything that infringes on constitutional rights must be challenged.

Thus, we must object when one of the parties argues in the opening argument. We must also object when reference is made to excluded evidence or proof, such as in cases of searches that violate constitutional guarantees or statements from the pretrial stage that cannot be presented at the oral trial due to the absence of the witness.

Another valid reason to object is when the litigant provides an excessive explanation of the legal theories. For example, they may mention that they will base their position on unimpeachability under Article 34, but they cannot develop each requirement or its relevance at that point. That discussion is reserved for the closing argument. In this case, the objection would be based on the grounds that they are "arguing about the law, doctrine, and case law or how they should be applied."

The opening argument is a fundamental tool for lawyers in an oral trial. In it, we present our side of the story based on facts, rights, and evidence to persuade the judge and jury. However, this pleading can also be subject to objections. This occurs when the litigant mentions facts not supported by evidence or misrepresents the truth. We may object if the meaning of the evidence is distorted, such as when testimony is claimed to support certain facts that, in fact, do not. It is crucial to challenge this misrepresentation immediately to avoid confusion among jurors.

Likewise, we may object if an interpretation is given that is contrary to what is established by law, doctrine, and jurisprudence. On the other hand, we object to the closing argument when unproven facts are mentioned, or the result of the facts, the evidence, or the law is misrepresented. Similarly, it is relevant to note that the personal opinions of counsel are completely irrelevant in a trial, as they do not constitute evidence of value. Their inclusion may lead to confusion about the relevance of the arguments at trial and their evidentiary basis.

Ultimately, mastery of objections at oral trials is essential to ensure clarity, fairness, and efficiency in the presentation of evidence. These strategic tools strengthen the integrity of the judicial process and ensure a fair representation of the facts in dispute.

Objection to the judge:

What happens when the judges are not willing to give up their role as investigators, which they have fulfilled for so many years under the inquisitorial process, and begin to interrogate? And, if they wish, only then do they give us the floor.

This situation is more common than it should be and really puts us in a situation in which we are not very clear about what we should do.

The question we usually ask ourselves is: Is it valid to object to the judge? What consequences could it bring us? Do we object only when it suits us?

We are really presented with a dilemma to which no single answer can be given; it will depend on how confident you are in your case and how much courage you have to mark the court with the judge (who seems to be your rival).

It is a difficult decision to make, but in our profession, every decision involves a risk, and it is smart to take them in time.

On one occasion, I experienced a situation similar to the one described above. The judge, a university professor in litigation, began the trial in which I was to represent the defendant accused of crimes against the freedom of persons, specifically the crime of human trafficking.

Every time a witness for the defense sat down to testify, the judge was the one who questioned first, and when he gave us the floor, he used to interrupt my performance because he questioned the answers given by our witnesses.

So, the cards being dealt, I had to act, and I asked him to send the witness out because I had to make a statement to the magistrate. I tried to be cordial and polite, as the last thing I wanted was to turn the magistrate against me.

However, despite my request, it was not granted, and the magistrate insisted that I formulate my arguments in the presence of the witness.

You can imagine the tense moment we lived through, my assistant and I.

It was then that with legal arguments, I asked the court to give me the opportunity to ask me first when it came to witnesses offered by my side, as indicated by the procedural rule, and if any doubt remained about the answer, of course, I could clarify.

This request did not cause any thanks, and the magistrate defended his position. However (and I refer to the facts), I must say that he then corrected his performance and allowed me to ask first.

The exercise of the leadership role often requires confronting authority with nobility.

PROFESSIONAL ADVICE

- ★ *Objecting is an art that we must practice in order to develop it properly.*
- ★ *Objecting requires a higher degree of attention on our part.*
- ★ *We must do it out loud, as we only have a fraction of a second to be awake and do our job properly.*
- ★ *We do not have to object for the simple fact of doing so and risk damaging our reputation.*
- ★ *We strategically target according to the plan.*
- ★ *The first thing to look at is whether the question hurts our theory of the case.*
- ★ *Evaluate whether the constitutional rights of the party I represent are being affected.*
- ★ *Control the information introduced by the adversary at the same time it occurs.*
- ★ *We must object to the intention to introduce pernicious or damaging information in the sense that it may generate a stigma on the parties involved.*
- ★ *Remember that there are many kinds of objections available to the litigator to do an excellent job.*

CLOSING ARGUMENT: THE ART OF PERSUASION IN LITIGATION

"Safety is the most seductive weapon of all. Powerful in front of the court".

Fabian was the lawyer in that case. The plaintiff, Cristina, had asked her friend Martin to recommend a good criminal lawyer since her case had been elevated to trial.

Cristina hired Fabian on Martin's advice, paid his fees, and gave him a copy of the entire file. Cristina was a plaintiff and had a lawyer, but he decided to resign because he did not feel ready to act in court.

Fabian was a university professor, in addition to being in charge of practical subjects for students at a major university. He boasted of being the most expert, with dozens of oral trials to his credit.

When Cristina asked him about the strategy of his trial, he responded with airs of grandeur, saying that he already had everything clear and not to worry.

Cristina was not satisfied with that answer and asked for more information. She also felt somewhat nervous and anxious because, in that trial, she had to face her aggressor, Fabian, who did not meet with her or her witnesses.

In a phone call that lasted 5 minutes, he asked her a question, and without listening to the complete answer, he knew what Cristina was going to testify the following day.

With respect to the witnesses, he proceeded in the same manner.

The trial started, and Fabian decided not to present his opening argument. Cristina did not understand much about the mechanics of the process, so she almost did not notice it.

Then, it was Cristina's turn to testify; she was nervous. Fabian asked her 2 or 3 questions, the judges questioned her, and the lawyer of the accused invaded her with questions, which she answered truthfully but which took her by surprise.

Fabian seemed overwhelmed and somewhat rushed, so much so that he decided to dismiss several witnesses who favored his accusation.

The experts came by and gave their statements; Fabian asked 2 or 3 questions only.

It was time to plead, and first, Fabian had to do it. He did not have his argument written down; he did not remember the names of the witnesses, much less the names of the experts. While he was presenting (almost in an improvised manner), he searched in the folder for the information and the data he did not remember; he asked his client, Cristina, for it. The court was becoming impatient.

Fabian then spun some sentences and said that the facts of threats should be considered proven on two occasions, but the complaint was for three and accused of simple threats when, in fact, according to Cristina, they were death threats, that is to say, aggravated.

Cristina lost her case, and she was totally disappointed, not only by the outcome but by the lackluster performance of Fabian, who not only failed to prepare as was his responsibility but also proved to be unprofessional despite the great reputation that supposedly preceded him.

Believe it or not, the case in question reflects a real event.

Unfortunately, there are many improvised lawyers who boast of their specialty of their degrees but do not honor our profession.

Remember that you can disguise your ineptitude during the direct and counter exams, but in the closing argument, everything will come out, including how unprepared you were to do it.

Fabian, like many others, collaborated with his poor performance to contribute to the bad concept that many have of our work.

This is why I often say that justice depends largely on us; on our performance. Cristina, with the help of another lawyer, could have obtained a valuable result for her life and safety.

Do not forget the case cited as an example, and remember that the closing argument is the presentation of your masterpiece, so prepare yourself with time and assume your role with responsibility and care.

The moment of fame has arrived...

At the end of the evidentiary phase, that is, when both parties have conducted their respective examinations and cross-examinations, it is necessary for the litigants to request the floor to present their final conclusions about the probative value of the evidence contained in the file and that which has been presented live during the trial.

Despite the fact that in many procedural systems, it is considered that the presentation of pleadings is a power of the lawyer and not an obligation, my emphatic advice is to take advantage of this opportunity. Why? Because this is your only chance to provide a detailed explanation of the evidence, recall the main thesis of the case, and make a specific request. I believe that as a litigator, you have a moral responsibility to do so if you are truly committed to your client, his cause, and the defense of the rights you represent.

While it is true that in some procedural systems, written pleadings are allowed to be submitted after a set time limit, we cannot fail to emphasize that this practice undermines the fundamental purpose of an oral hearing. The principles of immediacy, contradiction, and publicity, pillars of the judicial system, clearly demonstrate that the litigant should not miss the opportunity to be in front of the judges to explain why his position should prevail.

Now, consider the litigator who has spent time and effort researching his case, has thoroughly prepared every question asked during the oral hearing, has objected to adversarial questions, and has proposed key witness questions to support his theory of the case. After so much work, it would be unthinkable for you not to take advantage of this procedural tool to set forth, in your own words, all the details of the facts and the parties' involvement in them.

Let us also think of the judges, who have supervised every piece of evidence, issued orders, invested time in the matter, and, after listening for a long day to the parties and witnesses in oral argument, are obliged to form their own conclusions in order to issue a judgment. They also wish to hear the litigant's conclusions and hear the litigant's wishes. This may or may not coincide with the initial claims presented in the complaint or answer.

In addition, it is crucial that the judge hears directly from the litigant what adjustments he should consider in his claims after the evidence is presented, remembering that the evidence may or may not support the position of both parties.

On some occasions – and depending on the procedural system – the judge may issue his ruling immediately, while on others, he is granted an extended period of time to do so (which may affect the principle of immediacy). In either case, he or she must recall the statements of each witness and expert, analyze the file, and evaluate the positions of the parties to determine who is in the right. This process is significantly facilitated when the attorney presents his or her conclusions at the hearing.

The closing argument represents the most momentous argumentative exercise in the legal process. In this instance, we communicate to the court how our version of the facts has been proven and why it should be considered the definitive narrative that supports the judgment we seek. Effectively, the litigant presents his or her argument as if he or she were outlining the judgment itself; it is an oral projection to the judge or court, who will then step back and take into account what is expressed during these final words.

However, it is important to note that the quality of our pleading depends to a large extent on the diligence and competence demonstrated at all previous stages of the process. If our performance has been deficient up to this point, we are likely to have little solid material to present in our closing arguments.

The pleading is not an exercise in empty rhetoric nor a mere repetition of case law or legal doctrine. It is neither an academic lecture nor a theatrical performance.

I have seen throughout my professional career all types of lawyers. There are those who are too histrionic, who do not stick to the evidentiary material collected in the trial but make a real drama of a theatrical scene, and who try to show off, forgetting what the purpose of pleading is.

There are also those who have participated very little during the trial, but when the time comes to argue, they stand up confidently and are precise and eloquent in expressing their objectives.

We should also mention those who are afraid that their memory will play tricks on them, and so they read their pleadings from beginning to end, forgetting that pleading is an act of communication and, as such, should involve the recipients of the message.

Others, who have pretended to be very prepared during the trial, but when the time comes to speak, they do not have much to say; they do not remember the names of the parties or experts, and they show that they have no basis to defend a position, simply because they have been lazy.

But there are those who we all want to listen to, whether they are right or wrong, whether they win or lose that trial. These litigants are those who have acted with passion and conviction throughout the process, have captured the attention from the beginning, have stood up to arbitrariness, and have taken the gamble when questioning each witness and expert witness. They are the litigators who, when they take the floor, know what to say, in what order to say it, and who also have the ability to simplify technicalities. These litigators took the case seriously and were willing to give their best until the last minute.

Of course, there are many ways to plead, but each and every one of us must recognize that we can do better. Let us then look at some issues that will help us meet such objectives.

Pleading involves the ability to establish a coherent connection between the position of the party we represent, the facts we have presented, the evidence that supports them, and the arguments we develop.

The objective is to allow the judge to understand and accept our perspective, persuading him/her through a solid and convincing argumentation.

The act of arguing at trial represents the culmination of an exhaustive and essential process in our work as lawyers, our work on the case. At this point, we consolidate our theory of the case and make strong arguments that support the objectives we have pursued from the outset of our representation in court. This act ultimately defines the course of our performance in the judicial process.

Thus, the pleading constitutes our final offensive, a masterful synthesis of all the actions undertaken throughout the process. It is a powerful and moving narrative that cuts through each phase, offering a logical and coherent explanation that is in line with common sense and, of course, based on the existing legal framework. This is the unique and perfect opportunity to highlight our strengths and candidly address our weaknesses, all with the ultimate goal of persuading the court that our version of the facts is the most accurate and fair, thus meriting the endorsement of the final judgment.

In what forms is the pleading presented?

The act of standing up offers several advantages, such as the comfort of moving easily and using the body as a communication tool.

In terms of the manner in which the pleading is done, it is important to aim for the possibility of standing up. This allows for the expression of emotions and, on occasion, the use of objects to highlight crucial evidence. In case the judges are not accustomed to this practice, it is appropriate to ask their permission.

Regardless of whether you choose to make your closing remarks standing or sitting, the key is to convey assurance, confidence, and conviction in your words. The key to communicating this conviction is to speak with firmness and authority, and to achieve this; you must repeatedly practice until you feel comfortable and confident.

Closing arguments represent the ideal time for the lawyer to stand out, showing commitment to the case and providing solid reasons to support his or her request. It is not only about the requirements necessary to make a persuasive argument but also about the essential elements for effective communication between the litigant and his or her audience, whether it is the judge or the jury.

In any trial, there are usually at least two competing versions of the facts, and only one of them will prevail. Therefore, the pleading is considered a tool that allows the lawyer to maintain the faith that his client placed in him by entrusting him with the case.

On the other hand, we must overcome the idea of a superficial orality, in which we are present only out of obligation and not because we understand the benefits of verbal communication.

> *Another important recommendation is to avoid reading during the pleading. Pleading by reading from a paper can convey coldness and is, therefore, rarely effective.*

The litigant's presence at the trial should not only be physical but he or she must also demonstrate that he or she is fully engaged. That is, strive to create an atmosphere conducive to having your words resonate in the courtroom and be well received. While this approach can be challenging, it is essential to understand the opportunity presented. By expressing himself or herself orally, without relying on paper, the lawyer can channel the emotions that the case generates, emphasize relevant aspects, and strengthen the link to the values he or she seeks to highlight.

Let's take the case of our everyday life, such as a meeting in which a dialogue is initiated. In this case, we would not consider relying on a piece of paper when interacting, but rather, we communicate verbally while looking our interlocutor in the eyes. For, in the same way, a trial is a kind of dialogue between the lawyer and the judge, albeit with formalities and a more solemn tone. However, it is still an act of communication.

Although oral argument requires more effort on the part of the litigant, it carries greater rewards. If you ever doubt whether it is worth it, remember to consider the cost versus the benefit.

Verbal and nonverbal language in pleadings

➢ *Body language, its importance, and its relationship to litigation.*

In the collective mindset, lawyers are often seen as charismatic individuals, and at times, they are attributed with a certain air of mystery, as if they are always ready to litigate in any imaginable context. There is a perception that they must be knowledgeable on a wide range of subjects, regardless of their colleague's specialty or the area in which they are asked for an opinion. However, it is also a fact that people have varied opinions about lawyers, sometimes due to previous negative experiences or stereotypes ingrained in popular culture.

Whether fair or unfair, the image that people have of lawyers in the 21st century is relevant, as this perception directly influences their trust in the justice system. Therefore, it is crucial that we act as professionals committed to our work and follow the rules and values that make a person considered trustworthy. For we are the defenders and doers of justice; that is our role in society.

It is also important to remember that people, including lawyers, constantly communicate not only through our words but also through our gestures and body language. In fact, the simple act of not speaking or remaining silent does not imply that we are not communicating. Therefore, we must be mindful of our actions both in court and in out-of-court situations, such as mediation hearings, as our nonverbal language can convey messages just as powerful as our words.

In short, the way we present ourselves and conduct ourselves not only affects our personal reputation but also influences the general public's perception of the justice system. As advocates of this system, it is our duty to act with integrity and professionalism at all times, both in words and actions.

➢ *Litigants: key players in the pleadings*

Litigators must master control of their face, hands, and overall posture. The reason is clear: as lawyers, we are vested with the responsibility to embody the utmost professionalism and trustworthiness. The representation of justice is a serious task that must be treated with the seriousness it deserves.

The Mehrabian rule states that verbal language, that is, the language that comes out of our mouth, contributes only 7% to the communication of emotions and feelings, while 38% corresponds to paraverbal language (intonation, projection, tone, emphasis, pauses, rhythm, etc.), and a significant 55% to body language (gestures, postures, movements, breathing, etc.).

Therefore, it is imperative for any lawyer participating in an oral hearing to master this tool for effective communication. This involves, among other things, building confidence at the beginning of the presentation and maintaining it throughout the process.

The key to successful communication lies not only in the message that is conveyed but also in whether that message reaches the recipient as planned. If the message arrives distorted or is not understood, it is an indication that a poor job has been done or that body language has not been used correctly. Sometimes, a single false move or inappropriate word can have detrimental consequences and ruin all the previous work.

Participating in oral hearings is a special challenge. In that context, litigants do not have the chance to flip through their documents to find answers, review the law, or check the names of witnesses. There is no room for improvisation.

In front of the judges, the opposing party, the public, and, in particular, his client, the litigator must demonstrate a deeper knowledge of the case than anyone else in the courtroom. This confidence must not only manifest itself through words but must also be reflected in his or her body language, which must be carefully selected.

The body speaks for us, even when we are silent. It often reveals what we are trying to hide. Therefore, the litigator must use his body language precisely, as all eyes are on him, and he is the center of attention.

That said, emotional preparation is essential to face this challenging scenario. The litigator must anticipate the tense exposure he or she is about to face. The time has come when lawyers participating in an oral hearing cannot hide behind mountains of paperwork; it is time to become the director and protagonist of the story they intend to tell.

Components of nonverbal language in pleadings

Effective communication is a skill that transcends words, and the field of law is no exception. The way a lawyer presents and communicates, both verbally and nonverbally, can be the key to conveying confidence, persuasiveness, and control in the courtroom.

- *The language of the body*

Maintain an upright posture, with your head held high and shoulders back. This projects confidence and self-assurance.

Avoid standing with slumped shoulders, head down, or hands in pockets, as this may suggest a lack of confidence.

Before you begin your argument, wait until the room is quiet to make sure your words do not go unnoticed.

- *The importance of the look*

Watch the judges or members of the court as you speak to them, and observe their reactions and facial expressions. This will allow you to tailor your speech according to their nonverbal responses.

The gaze is a powerful tool for capturing attention, but avoid overly intense eye contact, as this can be intimidating.

- *Use of hands*

Your hands can be valuable allies in communication. Showing the palms of your hands suggests honesty and reasonableness.

Putting your hands together in the shape of an ogive can symbolize the connection between your arguments and what justice represents.

A gentle hand movement, as if painting in the air can be thought-provoking.

In contrast, clenching your fist or making sudden movements can convey anger or frustration, which can be effective in illustrating injuries or grievances in your argument.

- *The power of tone of voice*

Your tone of voice reveals your emotional state, whether it is confidence or fear. Use it strategically: changing your tone or pausing your speech can emphasize key points and build suspense in your narrative.

Make sure your voice is clear and audible without mumbling or hesitation. Open eyes and eye contact can help maintain focus.

Verbal and nonverbal language is a crucial tool for the practice of oral litigation and lawyering in general. It is not only what you say but also how you say it and how you present it. Mastering these skills, in addition to helping you gain the confidence of others in the courtroom, will also strengthen your ability to persuade and control the narrative of your case, thus achieving success in court.

Objectives of the Closing Argument

The fundamental purpose of the closing argument is clear and compelling: to persuade and convince the members of the court that, in rendering their judgment, they should consider you as the undisputed winner in this case. It is a unique opportunity to argue exhaustively on all aspects of the case and to unite them into a coherent and solid conclusion in support of your motion.

Imagine the closing argument as the denouement of a movie. The litigant has the task of reminding the court of everything he has witnessed as if he were narrating the denouement of a plot. It is at this point that we must tie up loose ends, i.e., explain evidence that may not have been entirely clear during the trial. The goal is to present the judge with a finished work, ready for his or her appreciation.

During the closing argument, we must address several essential aspects:

➢ **The Motto-Theme**

Recall that, in developing the theory of the case, we assign a title that identifies and relates the facts to moral standards, ethics, principles of justice, and, of course, to the law. This choice is not only strategic; it is also used during the trial. Here, you can present your case to the court, saying something like, "Your Honors, this case is about..." and then pronounce your motto. For example, you might refer to "the underdog" or "the importance of listening to children when no one else did."

I recommend that you repeat the slogan at some crucial point in your presentation so that it sticks in the court's mind. This is critical to emotionally bind the judges to your case and your client. Remember, the goal is to evoke empathy and understanding, inviting judges to fulfill the noble mission of lawyering: to bring social peace and dignity to people's lives through justice.

➢ **The facts**

When we talk about litigation techniques, we mention the usefulness of working with a theory of the case to establish our position. However, in court, we cannot refer to this theory. Instead, we must speak of proven, concrete facts.

At this stage, you should present your version of how the events occurred, whether your client was involved or not, and whether responsibility can be attributed to your client or whether the fault lies with someone else. Remember, you are not issuing an opinion; you are explaining your version supported by concrete evidence.

➢ Credibility of witnesses

When assessing the credibility of witnesses at trial, it is essential to consider not only the answers given during their testimony but also personal circumstances that may influence their objectivity. Although all procedural systems include so-called "general questions of law," which are standard questions asked of witnesses to determine whether they have any type of relationship with the parties, such as friendship, enmity, kinship, or interest in the outcome of the trial, it is essential to consider not only the answers given during their testimony but also the personal circumstances that may influence their objectivity.

However, as experienced litigators, we know that, in most cases, witnesses tend to answer "no" to these standard questions, with rare exceptions. This initial denial does not guarantee that there is no link between the witness and the proposing party. It is important to remember that relationships may have arisen before or after the events in question.

Therefore, it is incumbent upon us, the litigants, to explore these circumstances, both before and after the disputed incident. Why? Because these relationships can have a significant impact on the perception of the witness and, therefore, on his or her credibility.

> If *it is discovered that the witness concealed or distorted the truth about the nature of his or her relationship with any of the parties, this may affect their credibility and give rise to arguments against him or her.*

If it is a witness that we present, it is critical to emphasize why the court should find his or her testimony credible. For example, if the witness is a work colleague or friend of the plaintiff, we must explain why his or her testimony should not be affected by this relationship. We must emphasize that, beyond any relationship, the witness witnessed the events and can provide crucial details about the circumstances, time, and place, all critical elements in placing the witness in the context of the events.

When we refer to what the witness has stated in his or her testimony, it is essential to quote his or her words verbatim whenever relevant. This strategy not only shows our fidelity to the witness's original statement but also lends additional weight to our argument. For example, we can briefly interrupt our presentation and say: "Your Honors, let me quote verbatim from the witness Rodolfo, who stated: 'Alberto was drunk and could not even stand up.' This strengthens our case since we are faithful to the witness's statement before all those present at the hearing. The judges heard it and can verify our assertions, which can help support our credibility. However, this strategy should be used with caution and only in exceptional situations.

Occasionally, we need to call on the assistance of experts to address technical or complex issues. For example, they can help us understand the mechanics of an incident, authenticate documents, or interpret medical test results. The reasons for using an expert witness can vary widely.

At the time, we must address an expert's testimony and present arguments that support or question his or her credibility and suitability. If we are in favor of the expert's testimony, we can highlight his or her professional experience, academic training, and specialized knowledge that distinguishes him or her in his or her field. On the other hand, if we wish to challenge his testimony, we must address the reasons why the judge should question his opinion. This may be due to the expert's lack of updating in his area of expertise or inconsistencies between his trial testimony and what he has written in his previous publications.

At this point, in analyzing the expert testimony, we should not simply quote the expert's conclusions in a generic way. Instead, we should explain how the expert testimony supports our theory of the case or why it should be challenged. For example, rather than simply stating that the expert concluded that the accident was John's fault, we must provide a detailed explanation of the mechanics of the events and how these conclusions do or do not align with our position. Judges expect clear and convincing answers to these questions.

➢ **Proof of material**

At this stage, we refer to material evidence, specifically documentary or informational evidence that has been gathered throughout the written process. The key to a lawyer's ability to use this evidence persuasively is not to simply recite dates or transcribe responses from entities. Rather, it is essential to relate this evidence to the facts of the case.

Consider the following example: suppose we wish to prove both the time when an accident occurred and the direction of travel of the vehicles involved. We have documentary evidence that can provide relevant information. For example, we can have in our possession and present in the file the receipt of a parking lot located on Juncal Street. This parking lot is where the defendant usually leaves his vehicle on Thursday nights when he goes out to dinner with friends. In addition, this parking lot is located right across the street from the restaurant they go to.

In the pleading, we could argue the following: *"Ramiro, who is used to going out for fun every Thursday with his friends, with whom he has dinner and several glasses of wine, as the waiter of the place told us, usually leaves his car in the garage on Juncal Street, right in front of the restaurant. This saves him from having to walk a few blocks if he has had a few too many drinks. We have the ticket from that parking lot, which tells us about what happened that night. Ramiro picked up his car at 11 o'clock at night, and tired, he drove for more than a kilometer at high speed until he collided with my client at the intersection with Patricios Street, who didn't even have the reflexes to brake."*

In this case, we are demonstrating several crucial aspects, including the reason for Ramiro's departure, his company that night, his actions prior to the event, his conditions when taking the car, the moment he removed the vehicle, and the distance he traveled. In addition, we could have incorporated other informal evidence, such as communications through social networks (Facebook, Instagram) or WhatsApp conversations. While this evidence may be controversial, it is important to explicitly mention why it was presented and what purpose it serves in the context of the case.

In summary, the pleading must trace a complete path through all the evidence presented in order to provide a coherent and convincing explanation. In addition, it is essential to address the relevant technical issues, as detailed below.

➢ Legal argumentation and effective use of law

Mentioning a specific article of the Civil Code or labor law, for example, does not constitute evidence in itself. The litigant must articulate how the case fits the law and that particular article, presenting strong arguments to support his interpretation as opposed to his opponent's position. He must provide the court with sound reasons for applying the law in the way he proposes rather than in the way suggested by the opposing party. This involves more than mere citation; it requires reasoned argumentation.

It is advisable to refer to case law, but again, it is not enough to cite it superficially. The litigant must explain why this case law is relevant to its case and why it should influence the court's decision. If the litigant intends to depart from a body of case law, he or she should provide strong arguments supported by specific facts to justify his or her position.

The discussion of evidentiary burdens is crucial at this stage. The litigant must address who had the burden of proving certain facts and whether or not this burden was met. Even if he was at a disadvantage, it is important to highlight any evidence he has presented to support his position.

Knowledge of the law is essential, both in terms of the aspects favorable to your case and in relation to the rights that the opposing party is invoking. You must demonstrate a thorough and solid understanding of the legal framework surrounding the dispute.

In addition, it is essential to effectively refute all arguments presented by the opposing party. This should not be surprising if you have been attentive during the trial and have closely followed the development of the case. A skilled litigator should anticipate the counterarguments that the other side might present in relation to its case, its evidence, and the law it invokes.

Likewise, it is imperative to remember that judges are aware that they must make decisions in cases with opposing positions. Therefore, it is the lawyer's responsibility to argue in his or her own favor. Successful argumentation lies in the ability to effectively present one's position, rebut the opposing arguments, and provide the court with a sound basis for its decision.

➢ Clearly presenting the petition

When you reach this crucial stage of the process, it is very important that you formulate your requests explicitly and clearly. Often, some litigants tend to assume that their wishes are self-evident and do not need to be expressed out loud, but this is not the right approach.

When addressing the court, it is essential to state unequivocally what you are seeking to have resolved. Avoid ambiguities and make sure your request is precise and concise. For example, if you represent the plaintiff: *"Your Honor, everything we have witnessed during the trial compels us to ask you to condemn Juan as responsible for the accident."*

If he represents the defendant: *"Your Honor, Juan would have liked to avoid the accident, but he could not because it was Pedro who was driving over the allowed speed, in an absolutely reckless manner and unconcerned about the damage that could be caused. Therefore, we request that the claim be rejected with the imposition of costs to the plaintiff".*

No relevant aspect should be left to chance. If the litigant is clear about what he is seeking and to what extent, he should communicate this precisely to the court. This ensures that his objectives are properly recorded and also demonstrates his professionalism and understanding of the case to the court.

Organization of the closing argument: Good practices

Be prepared to communicate effectively and use time wisely.

1. ***Use time effectively***
➔ *Consider your audience.*
➔ *Make efficient use of time to respect limited attention.*
➔ *Direct the presentation to what really matters for the case.*

2. ***Advance preparation***
➔ *Write the plea on paper to organize your thoughts.*
➔ *Create an outline or list of main ideas.*
➔ *Be prepared to speak fluently without relying on written notes.*

3. ***Makes an impact from the start***
➔ *Start straightforward and without digressions.*
➔ *Use a relevant tagline to make an impact from the start.*
➔ *Plan how to refer back to the slogan throughout the pleading.*

4. ***Summarizes key evidence***
➔ *Highlight relevant evidence to support your point of view.*
➔ *Report who testified, what they said, and how they contributed to the case.*

5. ***Addresses weaknesses***
➔ *Strategically explain the weaknesses of the case.*
➔ *Anticipate and counteract possible offensives by the adversary.*

6. ***Ignore unimportant facts***
➔ *Discern between relevant and inconsequential facts.*
➔ *Keep the focus on crucial aspects of the case.*

7. ***Appeals to emotions***
➔ *Convey your customer's experiences and feelings.*
➔ *Highlight the impact of the case on the client's life.*
➔ *Use concrete and contextual examples.*

8. ***Law enforcement***
➔ *It links the case to the law in a clear and precise manner.*
➔ *Avoid excessive technical explanations.*
➔ *It ends with a shocking statement related to the law.*

9. ***Justify the desired verdict***
➔ *Motivate the court to render a verdict in your favor.*

→ *Explain why your request is fair and based on the facts and the law.*
→ *Conclude in a respectful and convincing manner.*

*10. **Farewell***
→ *Justify your action or defense.*
→ *Demonstrate reasonableness and absence of excesses in your requests.*
→ *Clearly identify the desired result.*

→ Use time effectively

The presentation of a closing argument is an art that is not governed by rigid or standardized formulas. Each litigant has his or her own style and approach, and this freedom is essential. However, there are some general guidelines that can serve as a guide.

First, consider your audience, i.e., the people who will listen to your plea. Imagine it as a gift you are offering and ask yourself what they would like to receive. This approach helps direct your presentation toward what really matters to your case.

One of the most effective ways to show respect for the audience is to make efficient use of time. People's time and attention are limited resources, so do not abuse them. The length of the argument may vary depending on the complexity of the issue, but regardless of that, avoid unnecessary beating around the bush and get straight to the point. This shows that you know what you are talking about and that you have resolved what you set out to communicate.

Remember that the judges are there to hear something relevant, so be sure to deliver it clearly and concisely. Also, your client expects to see it represented in your words; this is an opportunity to show them how hard you have worked on their behalf.

→ Make your preparation in advance

Preparation is key to presenting a closing argument without relying on written notes. And since the goal is to speak fluently without relying on paper, it is essential to prepare in advance.

The first recommended step is to write your pleading on paper. This will allow you to organize your thoughts according to the essential requirements, such as stating the facts, relating them to the evidence, and grounding your petition in the law. This also ensures that you do not forget any crucial points during your presentation.

Then, on a separate sheet of paper, you can create a sort of outline or list of the main ideas you plan to convey. This could take the form of a chart or a timeline. Feel free to use this sheet as a guide during your presentation, not to read it verbatim, but as a visual reminder of the key points.

In fact, preparing in advance will not only help you feel more confident during your closing argument but will also ensure that you do not overlook important details in your presentation. Remember, practice and preparation are essential to success in the art of the closing argument.

➔ Makes an impact from the start

In the preparation of your closing statement, you should consider, among other things, how your presentation will begin. It is crucial not to ramble on or waste the first few minutes on empty words or unnecessary thank yous. Instead, it is imperative to be direct from the start. Ask yourself the question: what do I want the judge to remember at the end of my presentation? Then, go directly to answering that question.

An effective technique is to start strong by using your tagline if it is relevant to their case. Remember that people tend to remember the first and last things they hear, so it is essential to make an initial impact. Next, consider when and how you will mention your slogan again throughout your pleading, linking it to testimonials, experts, or other probative evidence. Your slogan should be consistently linked to the facts and evidence.

Likewise, it is vital to plan what you will say second and third, making sure they are logically connected. Try to paint vivid pictures with your words so that they stick in the judge's mind. In addition, you can determine what documents or visual evidence you might use to support and enrich your presentation.

➔ Summarizes key evidence

Facts, by themselves, lack validity without evidence to support them. Therefore, it is critical to highlight the evidence that supports your point of view. It is not necessary to address all of the evidence presented unless it is particularly relevant to your strategy.

Inform the judge who testified and what they said, remembering why you called those witnesses in the first place and how their testimony contributes to the case. By recalling the exact words of the witnesses, they take on special force and meaning. Remember, it is your responsibility to show how the evidence supports your argument and how it relates to the facts of the case.

➔ Addresses weaknesses

In any event, it is critical to strategically address any weaknesses that may arise. Every litigator must understand that perfect cases are a pipe dream in the real legal context; therefore, anticipation and explanation of why things did not go as planned are essential. These explanations are critical, as the omission of such explanations could lead the judge to suspect that information is being withheld or that events did not unfold as initially stated, which could undermine the credibility initially placed in the attorney.

Adverse evidence that is not addressed is left on its own, so it is not appropriate to leave such a relevant issue to the court's interpretation. Hence the importance of assuming the complexity of the case and presenting a logical alternative for its understanding.

It is imperative that you provide a reasonable explanation justifying the departure from the court's own case law. Likewise, you need to address the challenges and objections raised during the hearing or that are pending resolution. Discussing your client's reputation or the facts that do not favor him or her is crucial; explaining why, even though it is negative, you have a logical and credible explanation that can overturn the legal presumptions against him or her.

Remember that your weaknesses can become your opponent's strengths, so it is essential to anticipate the offensive that he might launch. Anticipation will allow you to counteract the detrimental effects that these weaknesses may cause you. Therefore, the recommendation is clear: anticipate.

➔ Ignore unimportant facts

Another valuable tip lies in the ability to discern between relevant and inconsequential facts. It is not necessary to exhaust time and resources by mentioning every date, name, or number presented as expert evidence. In fact, an abundance of detail can be counterproductive, as it diverts the attention of the trier of fact.

It is vital to keep the focus on the crucial aspects of the case. Highlight important dates and key words expressed by witnesses. Reinforce your message through simplification. Weighing what witnesses and experts have testified, as well as what you plan to express about their credibility and knowledge of the facts, is essential to an effective presentation.

➔ Appeals to emotions

Every legal action originates from a story with characters who have emotions and feelings that have led them to act in a certain way. It is vital that you convey to the court the concerns and difficulties your client has experienced during the process. Talk about how your client has suffered and how he or she feels affected by the situation. You can also highlight the hopes your client has for the outcome of the case.

Also, relate how this event has profoundly impacted your client's life, changing his or her perspective or teaching valuable lessons. You can also talk about how the resolution of the case could affect society at large.

When addressing these issues, use concrete and contextual examples. Your goal is to make the court empathize with your client and fully understand his or her situation. Be respectful but direct in addressing ethical and moral issues related to the case.

➔ Law enforcement

It is crucial to link the case to the law clearly and precisely. Show how your argument conforms to or differs from the relevant legal provisions. Avoid giving overly technical or lengthy explanations of legal issues. Instead, present your arguments in a concise and focused manner.

It is important to keep in mind that the judge already has a solid understanding of the law. Do not underestimate his or her understanding. Instead, show respect for their time. End this section with a powerful statement or a relevant and impactful sentence that reinforces your argument.

→ **Justify and express the verdict you wish to obtain**

In the final part of your presentation, motivate the court to render a verdict in your favor. Do not plead if you do not present solid arguments to support your position. Explain why your request is fair, based on the facts and the law. Relate your requests to the needs of the parties involved and society at large.

Try to emphasize that your request is reasonable and not driven by negative emotions or a desire for revenge. Rather, demonstrate that you are seeking a civilized and fair solution in accordance with values and legality.

Conclude your argument in a respectful but very convincing manner. First, justify your action or defense, establishing a clear connection between the facts and the law. Next, demonstrate that you have acted reasonably and without excess in your requests. Finally, clearly and responsibly identify the desired outcome.

As you depart, do so with the satisfaction of having presented your best arguments as a litigant, with the hope that the court will render a fair and just

PROFESSIONAL ADVICE

★ *Turn the case into something worth deciding that will make you an oral litigation artist.*

decision.

PREVIOUS STATEMENTS: AN ADVANTAGE IN YOUR STRATEGY

HOW AND WHY SHOULD THEY BE USED IN THE ORAL TRIAL?

They are a useful tool of oral litigation that allows us to reproduce the past to confirm our position.

Preliminary statements are accounts and statements made by witnesses regarding the facts, circumstances, or the defendants' participation in an event. These statements are made under oath before a public official and are essential to understanding the details of the case.

This issue is crucial for trial lawyers, as it represents one of the exceptions to the rule of orality, contradiction, and immediacy in judicial proceedings.

In an adversarial process, as opposed to a mixed inquisitorial one, the incorporation of evidence by reading is prohibited. In the latter system, the incorporation of testimony without the presence of the witness used to be allowed, which affected the principles of orality, immediacy, and contradiction. Testimonial records are usually written by police officers, which often introduces technical terms that do not belong to the witness, making it difficult to accurately interpret the facts.

In addition, these records often lack essential details about the witness, such as his or her physical condition, which can only be extracted during direct examination.

At the same time, this approach affects the fundamental rights of the defense at trial, due process, and the presumption of innocence. It is in this context that the accusatory process adopts a fairer stance, requiring face-to-face testimony during the oral trial.

Let us remember that the credibility of testimony lies in the details provided by the witness, which are fundamental for the construction of evidence in cases of relevance.

Pre-statements are an essential tool that strengthens your legal strategy and your pursuit of justice.

Recapitulation of the lawyer's work:

As a lawyer, you have gone through several stages before you get to trial. First, you researched your case, which means you know the witnesses who will testify in favor of your theory of the case, as well as those who will testify against you. You have researched and interviewed them, as suggested in oral litigation practices. However, it is important to remember that during the oral trial, events may not unfold exactly as you had anticipated.

During the examination of witnesses, your initial approach is to use open-ended questions directed to the witness who supports your theory of the case. At this stage, you should introduce the witness to the judge and members of the court to establish his or her credibility. You should answer general questions of law to demonstrate that the witness has no interest in the outcome of the trial.

Once you have established your credibility, you will proceed to address two main issues:

1. The first refers to **internal perception,** which addresses the witness's physical abilities, such as vision, hearing, and other senses.
2. The second aspect is **external perception,** which relates to the events themselves. This includes the visibility conditions, the timing of the events, and any other relevant contextual details at the crime scene.

Therefore, as a trial lawyer, you must understand how and in what context you can use prior statements you have in your file. This is crucial while cross-examining a witness, **even if you are the one who offered the witness as a witness.**

Types of pre-declarations:

Preliminary statements may also take the form of memoranda. These writings are prepared by the declarant himself and are attached to the file. This is usually done through a witness statement or under oath.

Past memory writings can vary from handwritten documents to private documents, administrative records, photographs, multimedia messages, and more. However, it is always necessary to authenticate them. This implies that the declarant, on whom this information is to be asserted, must recognize it as his or her own and confirm its relation to the facts under investigation, or such confirmation must come from a reliable source with verification capability.

The role of the deposition in litigation:

Why *use a prior declaration?*

The answer lies in the strategy you are pursuing. Pre-statements are considered a last option, used when the attorney cannot otherwise obtain crucial information to support his or her theory of the case.

What this means is that you cannot simply resort to these statements because you do not know what questions to ask. In fact, doing so would be prohibited and would be grounds for objection.

A strategic attorney makes the decision to use these statements by carefully weighing the benefits and disadvantages. The attorney understands that by resorting to these statements, the credibility of the witness will be affected, as judges and jurors may question his or her testimony.

The use of forward-looking statements involves a meticulous and analytical approach in which you must carefully evaluate the costs and benefits involved.

Reasons for using **pre-statements**

1. Refreshing the witness's memory

Target	*Method*	*Importance*
Strengthen key points of the theory of the case.	*Use prior statements to remind the witness of crucial information.*	*It contributes to the coherence and accuracy of the testimonies.*

2. Attacking the credibility of the witness

Scenario	*Lawyer's action*	*Importance*
When the witness presents contradictions or variations in his statements throughout the judicial process.	*Using prior statements to point out inconsistencies and question the credibility of the witness.*	*It challenges the reliability of the testimony and affects the court's perception of the testimony.*

➢ *Refreshing the witness's memory*

This is done in order to strengthen a specific point in your theory of the case. You can draw on these prior statements to help the witness remember crucial information.

➢ *Attacking the credibility of the witness*

Prior statements are useful when the witness contradicts himself or herself or provides different statements at different stages of the judicial process. In this situation, the attorney should take steps to address the issue.

I remember that hearing as if it were today since it was the first time I put this famous oral litigation technique into action.

I tell you the case: Viviana, my client Javier's ex-partner, had denounced him for physical violence and threatened her in an alleged context of gender violence.

On the other hand, my client denied the facts and provided me with important information about the reality of the events. For example, Viviana generated a scandal without any basis when Javier came home from work. Viviana made a scene of jealousy, after which she began to attack him with a kitchen tool, leaving him with injuries on both legs. Before finishing her dramatization, she took a bag and started to put away her belongings; Javier kept himself isolated to prevent the aggressions from starting again, after which Viviana left the home where they had lived together for 8 years, shouting and shouting, taking hidden among her belongings, the savings recently inherited by Ruben, an important amount of foreign currency.

Viviana's alibi consisted of striking the first blow, so she walked about ten blocks, then took a cab to go to the hospital, which was just around the corner from the house where she lived with Javier. There, she presented herself with some scratches on her face, alleging that Javier had assaulted her, the reason for which the hospital staff gave notice, and the investigation for domestic violence was initiated by the family judge, who quickly ordered Javier to be notified of the restraining order against him.

Meanwhile, a criminal case was also initiated against Javier, who, as we have already said in other chapters, nobody would believe that instead of being the victimizer in this story, Javier had been the victim of aggression, domestic violence, physical injuries and the theft of a large sum of money, in addition to the emotional swindle he had suffered and the false accusations that weighed against him.

Therefore, one of our tasks as lawyers was to prove that Viviana had artfully planned the steps she had to take to leave Javier totally absorbed and defenseless. I do not rule out, unfortunately, that a colleague had "commented" to her about the advantages obtained in the justice system by denouncing an alleged aggressor.

As a result of our investigation, we discovered, among other things, that upon leaving the apartment they shared, several neighbors saw her face to face without noticing any injury to Viviana's face.

But the most curious thing was to discover that in the midst of these accusations, supposedly injured, Viviana had decided to use the tickets that Javier had booked to travel together to celebrate their anniversary.

Staying at the hotel. All within a few days of the scandal and the complaint filed.

Viviana was so happy with the gift that was for both of them but that she apparently used alone. We found a publication in her Facebook profile through which she thanked Javier (with name and surname) for her gift: the publication said: "thank you, my love, for this gift, I love you," accompanied by a photograph in which Viviana's face could be appreciated and in the background the plane that would take her to the happy destination.

During the investigation stage, we accredited the reports of the travel company through which my client had purchased the airline tickets and booked the hotel, as well as the previously certified Facebook screenshots.

With these documents in hand, we proceeded to cross-examine Viviana, who first denied the existence of this trip, which she finally had to acknowledge.

But the most spectacular moment happened when we confronted her testimony with the publications taken from her Facebook profile (written from memory).

True declarations of love and a full-face photograph that did not reflect any of the injuries referred to in her complaint.

In this way, thanks to the previous investigation and use of previous statements, we were able to come face to face with Viviana and her lies, revealing the sad reality, which is that Javier had been the victim of a false accusation.

Thanks to our teamwork with Javier, we are pleased that he has been acquitted of the charges he unjustly faced.

Uses of previous statements

Refreshing the memory of the witness

One of the most common uses of pre-statements in court is to refresh a witness's memory. Imagine this situation: you are conducting a direct examination, and you are asking open-ended questions of one of the witnesses you have presented. However, you realize that this witness does not remember some key details. At this point, that's when you can fall back on previous statements.

It is worth clarifying that you cannot simply start reading aloud the witness's prior statement. Instead, you must demonstrate your theory of the case by narrating your witness's story and using the prior statements as support.

Here, I will explain the steps to follow:

➔ **Step 1.** Begin by showing that the witness has memory problems. The most effective way to do this is by asking close-ended questions about details that the witness cannot remember. For example, you might ask, *"What color was the car?"* to which the witness will respond, *"I don't remember."*

➔ **Step 2.** Now, establish that the witness made a prior statement in which he described the events with greater clarity and detail. This suggests that at the time he made that statement, the events witnessed were fresher in his memory, making them easier to recall.

➔ **Step 3.** The last step is to prove that the prior statement is a public document. The witness read it and signed it, leaving no doubt that it was the witness who had provided that statement in the first place. By showing this document at trial, you will refresh the witness's memory, which is critical to establishing your case strongly in court.

Exemplary dialogue

(A- Attorney/B- Witness)
A- What color was the car?
B- I don't remember.
A- Have you made a statement to the police station?
B-Yes
A- Did you tell the policeman what you saw?
B-Yes
A-This was immediately after the events happened?
B-Yes
A- Upon seeing the defendant flee the scene?
B-Yes
A- And you gave important information to the policeman who helped to capture him?
B- That's right.
A- Did you testify at the police station?
B- Yes
A- After testifying, did you read and sign the minutes?
B-Yes
A- If I showed you that statement, would you be able to recognize it?
B-Yes, of course

In this dialogue, you will appreciate that the attorney is employing leading questions, one of the exceptions allowed during direct examination. Once we have introduced the prior statement provided by the witness, we will proceed to ask whether this statement helped him or her recall the events witnessed more accurately.

Once we have established the usefulness of the document, we can move on to ask specific details, such as, *"What color was the car?"*The witness will respond by providing the color, in this case, "the car was red," which helps us fill in the gaps in their narrative.

After clarifying this, counsel may choose to conclude the direct examination or continue to explore other aspects of the testimony. It is important to note that we cannot reuse the prior statement for purposes of refreshing the witness's memory, as this could lead the judge and jury to question whether the witness actually witnessed the events.

Referring once again to the **past report**, the procedure to assert this evidence will be the same as the one we used in the previous statements.

Incorporation of information provided by the witness presented by the adverse party

Sometimes, witnesses may offer statements that, while favoring one theory of the case over another, contain information useful to our argument. We may use the witness's prior statement to show the facts from a different perspective or to highlight specific aspects that the witness does not recall during the trial, which casts doubt on the certainty of his or her testimony.

To evidence contradictions **during cross-examination.**

In this situation, the witness provides information that varies depending on who is questioning him/her. When detecting contradictions between the prior statements and the answers given during the oral trial, the lawyer must point this out. The judge and jury cannot identify these contradictions themselves, as they have not had access to the prior statements. Therefore, it is the lawyer's responsibility to highlight these discrepancies.

To do so effectively, the attorney must follow these steps:

- ➔ First, demonstrate that the witness is in error, confused, or contradicting himself.
- ➔ The witness will then be led through a series of questions that will take them back to the time when they made their previous statement, and subsequently, they will be asked to read aloud the specific section that is inconsistent with their current testimony.
- ➔ It is crucial that the witness read his or her own statement aloud so that the judge and jury can clearly perceive inconsistencies in his or her testimony.

This procedure is essential to maintain the integrity of the process and ensure that the testimony is as accurate as possible.

During the questioning or cross-examination of experts or experts

> *In the process of questioning or cross-examining experts, it is invaluable to make use of prior statements.*

Such statements may not only evidence contradictions but also help to highlight certain limitations in the scientific procedures followed by the expert.

Let us remember that the data contained in an expert's report are obtained through scientific methods that, although rigorous, are not infallible. In this sense, it is crucial to highlight these issues during the expert's interrogation since concluding guilt based on 30% doubt is not a fair practice.

In turn, the introduction of the report is handled in a similar manner to what we have previously discussed. The expert will be questioned about a specific piece of information in the report. If this data contradicts the current statements, the report will be presented for review. Subsequently, the expert will be asked if he/she acknowledges the report, if he/she wrote it, and if he/she signed it. Once the expert confirms his or her authorship, the attorney will ask the expert to read the relevant portion of the report to support the point in question.

It is important to note that it is not necessary to conclude the cross-examination in an argumentative manner by the litigant. Once the expert has read the highlighted section, you may continue with other topics of questioning or, if appropriate, conclude the round of questioning.

In situations where the expert uses technical and complex language in his or her testimony, as compared to the submitted report, the attorney may rely on prior statements and the report to clarify obscure, ambiguous, or difficult-to-understand points.

Demonstrate the **consistency of the witness.**

This strategy is used to demonstrate that a witness's statements have been consistent throughout the various stages of the judicial process. It is particularly useful when dealing with vulnerable witnesses, such as the elderly, whose perceptive conditions are often questioned due to their advanced age.

Accordingly, the witness's prior statements can be relied upon to support his or her credibility and strengthen his or her testimony, especially when opposing counsel attempts to challenge his or her perceptiveness due to advanced age. **Consistency in the witness's prior statements can be a powerful argument for maintaining his credibility.**

By way of summary:

☞ **Let us understand that the principles of the adversarial process impose a fundamental rule on us.**

Any source of information related to an event under investigation must appear in court and expose everything he or she has witnessed. Herein lies the essence of our work as trial lawyers: establishing the foundation of credibility.

☞ **When it comes time to cross-examine a witness, your main task is to demonstrate that there are solid reasons to believe their testimony, or failing that, that no such reasons can be found.**

The key lies in stressing the importance of conducting a thorough investigation and, of course, the importance of having a prior interview with the witness. This step is crucial to avoid unnecessary contradictions and conflicts during the interrogation.

☞ **A valuable tool in your arsenal is pre-statements.**

These can be used to demonstrate consistency or, conversely, inconsistencies in the witness's testimony, according to the strategy you are following at trial.

☞ **Expert reports also become valuable allies.**

They can be used to highlight key facts or evidence contradictions as you interact with experts during questioning or cross-examination.

Maintaining a clear strategy and a meticulous focus on credibility and consistency of testimony is essential on the road to litigation success.

Every step you take, from investigation to trial, should be geared toward strengthening your position and convincingly demonstrating the truth behind your theory of the case.

PROFESSIONAL ADVICE

"It analyzes the witness, his previous statements, opinions expressed in any media, and writings of past memory to find what seems to be untraceable.

- DH

INTRODUCTION OF MATERIAL EVIDENCE: THE POWER OF PROOF

HOW TO USE MATERIAL EVIDENCE TO MAKE AN IMPACT AND LEAVE AN UNFORGETTABLE IMAGE

The presentation of material evidence at oral trial is a fundamental tool for successful litigation. These evidentiary elements are crucial to proving perpetration, motive, and the relationship between the parties, as well as for establishing the credibility of witnesses and experts who will testify or have already testified at trial.

In this way, they will serve to disprove or ratify the statements made about the case in question and, ultimately, to support each party's theory of the case.

But what is material evidence?

Material evidence, as opposed to prior statements pertaining to witnesses, experts, and parties, refers to **objects or documents related** to the facts under investigation. These elements may be public or private instruments and play a crucial role in the oral trial.

The evidence does not speak for itself.
So, how do we make the evidence speak?

It is important to understand that material evidence does not convey value - clear and patent - to the judge and jury unless it is properly introduced. This requires that it be introduced during direct or cross-examination. This process applies to both experts and witnesses and follows fundamental principles governing this activity.

Guiding principles of this practice

Principle of Probation	*A trial attorney is free to incorporate any type of evidence he or she deems relevant to the facts at issue, the parties involved, their motivations, or even to question the credibility of witnesses. Therefore, each litigator, regardless of his or her affiliation, must compile his or her own set of information for the purpose of identifying all the elements that support his or her theory of the case.*
Principle of distrust	*This principle allows any assertion made by the parties involved to be challenged. In other words, what a litigant alleges is not considered evidence at trial unless it is subject to the rules of direct examination and cross-examination. These rules establish that all evidence presented at trial must be subject to confrontation and contradiction by the adversary.*

Based on these two fundamental premises, it is essential for a strategic lawyer to follow a carefully laid out plan when preparing witness and expert testimony. This involves the development of both direct examination, which seeks to establish credibility and facts in favor of your theory of the case, and cross-examination, which seeks to challenge the credibility and arguments presented by the other side.

The effective execution of this plan is crucial to present a strong and persuasive defense in court.

Similarly, the ability to present this material evidence at trial is an essential skill for any lawyer. It is largely up to the creativity and acumen of the litigator to find and use these elements to support his or her theory of the case. It is important to note that this material evidence must have been previously presented during the investigative stage, where it was authenticated, and the opposing party was given the opportunity to confront it. In other words, it is already in the trial file.

In this sense, we are going to explore a technique that will allow us to incorporate this material evidence in the oral trial through the testimony of a witness or expert witness.

Steps to achieve authentication

The degree of accreditation required will vary depending on the type of evidence we are dealing with. If we are talking about evidence found at a crime scene, it must meet rigorous standards, such as chain of custody, to be considered authentic. On the other hand, a fact of public notoriety, widely known and accepted by society, will require less verification.

However, when it comes to evidence gathered and presented by a litigant at an oral trial, the level of authentication is more rigorous. During the pretrial stage, several steps must be taken to demonstrate the witness's relationship to the exhibits presented.

→ **What does it mean to be a *suitable witness*?**

A suitable witness is one who has a direct and relevant relationship to the material evidence presented. This relationship is critical and becomes the central focus of the litigant during the oral trial.

The skill of the attorney lies in summoning witnesses who are suitable to establish and demonstrate the authenticity of the exhibits. In other words, **one must carefully choose the witnesses who can contribute to the accreditation of the material evidence.**

Successful presentation of material evidence at trial depends not only on finding and authenticating such evidence but also on the litigator's ability to effectively connect this evidence with suitable witnesses. Skill in this process is essential to building a strong and persuasive theory of the case.

Steps for effective introduction of material evidence:

1. Investigation stage

In this first stage, we will go into the investigation. We must introduce the material evidence before reaching the oral trial. This has a dual purpose: to establish its authenticity and veracity and to give the adversary the opportunity to confront it, object to it, or request its exclusion. It is essential to understand that you cannot surprise anyone at trial with new evidence.

To ensure a fair and equitable process, **parties cannot withhold information. They must present it during the pre-trial stages.** This stage is crucial to avoid surprises and ensure that everyone involved is playing by clear rules.

2. Pre-trial preparation stage

The second stage focuses on the preparation for the oral trial. Let's remember: We are not there to discover the truth but to prove it. Therefore, we need to know this: *how, when, where, and by whom.* A lawyer strategist determines which witness to subpoena and how to present material evidence. This is paramount, as the order of presentation is critical.

The adversarial process gives us the opportunity to interview witnesses prior to trial. During this pretrial interview, we must address the material evidence: the what, how, when, where, and how to express this information. Practice in introducing material evidence and preparing the witness for cross-examination is essential at this stage.

> *Information that our witness does not know cannot be introduced, as this constitutes false testimony and procedural malpractice.*

Likewise, during this preparation stage, we will also address strengths and weaknesses. Weaknesses may be related to:

- the collection of evidence,
- chain of custody,
- authenticity of public instruments,

- authorship of private instruments, among others.

This is why a leading litigator is prepared to face any scenario at trial.

Stage of the introduction of material evidence at oral trial

When faced with the task of questioning a witness at trial, a variety of techniques provided by direct examination must be employed. These techniques include open questions, closed questions, and, in specific cases, leading questions.

Through cross-examination, our primary objective is to demonstrate that the witness possesses sound and relevant knowledge about the exhibit we plan to present in court. Open-ended questions give us the opportunity to allow the witness to introduce valuable information.

➢ **Here are the key steps to follow during cross-examination to introduce material evidence:**

1. ***Establish the identity of the witness:*** the first step is to establish the identity of the witness as a reliable and credible person before the court.

2. ***Establish credibility:*** It is critical to demonstrate that the witness is a credible source of information. This includes their ability to recall and provide accurate details.

3. ***Proving knowledge about the object of evidence:*** during cross-examination, we must ensure that the witness has in-depth and specific knowledge about the object of evidence we wish to present. This will support the relevance of the material evidence to our case.

It is necessary to emphasize that material evidence can not only be used during direct examination but also plays a fundamental role in cross-examination.

The ability to effectively manage the introduction of material evidence at trial is a crucial component in supporting our theory of the case. Through strategic cross-examination, we will be able to effectively present this evidence to strengthen our arguments and achieve our stated objectives.

Why is the introduction of material evidence allowed at the oral trial?

Material evidence exerts a significantly more persuasive and lasting influence on the memory of judges and juries than words alone. These elements have the power to leave an indelible impression on the minds of those deciding the case, allowing them to visualize and relive the precise moments in which the events unfolded.

> The material evidence transports us to the heart of the events.

In the past, when the adversarial process was not in place, attorneys often requested that material evidence be presented before they could give it meaning and context during their closing argument.

Today, the dynamics are different, and it is essential to provide a detailed explanation of the material evidence: its content, its relationship to the witnesses, and its linkage to the litigant's theory of the case. These aspects are accomplished through the credentialing of the witness and his or her testimony. Once the evidence is introduced following these procedures, it is available and available to the litigant for use in the proceeding.

This means that once a qualified witness has authenticated the material evidence, it can be used again with other witnesses and experts without the need to repeat the accreditation process.

Evidence that does not meet the higher authentication condition.

But what happens when the litigant seeks to rely on evidence that does not meet this condition of high authentication? This can be public instruments, private documents, recordings, photographs, WhatsApp conversations, social media posts, and even physical items such as clothing.

In these cases, the accreditation steps are equally crucial. First, a competent witness must be presented. Next, the basis of knowledge that this witness possesses about the evidentiary item in question is established. Third, the specific piece of evidence is requested for production, first from opposing counsel and then from the witness, who must acknowledge it.

On the other hand, in relation to written documents, a reading is made, which may be total or partial, depending on the nature of the evidentiary element to be used.

This meticulous and strategic process ensures the proper presentation of evidence, regardless of its form or type, and contributes to the construction of a strong narrative.

Always remember that, as a litigator, every step you take in the evidence introduction process is critical to the success of your case. The ability to effectively use material and testimonial evidence is an art that can make all the difference in the pursuit of justice.

PROFESSIONAL ADVICE

- ★ *Plan which of the evidence you offered in the investigation stage will be used in the oral trial, keeping in mind the principles of immediacy and procedural economy. You will have to be very selective with the evidentiary elements, as well as with the most appropriate moments to be used. All these decisions are strategic and must be linked to the plan and theory of the case.*
- ★ *During the preliminary analysis, to determine the relevance of the material evidence, you must take into account the strengths and weaknesses of that decision. This means that you need to be prepared to attack and defend your adversary's statements about the material evidence.*
- ★ *It is important that you plan the questions you are going to ask the witness to introduce the evidence.*
- ★ *You don't have to leave the job of introducing material evidence to the end. Firstly, because it would give the judge and jury the idea that these elements are not so important, and secondly, because of the risk that you might forget to use them. You must analyze what would be the right moment to introduce the evidence, the moment when it will have the greatest impact on the court, and give more strength to your theory of the case.*
- ★ *The use of objects should fit the rhythm and content of your story.*

Let's remember that we use these objects because they make an impact; a picture is worth a thousand words, and they are more easily engraved in people's memories.

Highlighted examples of material evidence in action.

- ➢ *Victim: Priscila Molina*
- ➢ *Defendant: Juan Manuel*

Two very important items have been seized from a crime scene; one of them is a key ring with six keys and a medal, and the other is a small chain containing the initials JM found near the victim's body. These items were found by police officer Raul Rodriguez, who is testifying in the trial.

At this point, we are faced with two different factual propositions. The prosecution says that the chain belongs to the defendant, Juan Manuel since the initials match. The second of the seized items, according to the prosecution's understanding, also belonged to the defendant and had been given by the victim voluntarily.

The prosecution is going to summon the expert in charge of partially lifting the traces from the crime scene to establish the DNA match, by means of the fingerprint, with that of the accused.

On the other hand, the defense strategy will be to give another meaning to the same evidence. Regarding the little chain found, the defense will deny that it belongs to the accused and affirm that it actually belongs to the victim's brother, Juan Molina. Regarding the keys, the defense will try to challenge the trace evidence and the link they have with the defendant and will also allege that although they belong to their client, they were stolen from his workplace.

Prosecutor's interrogation of police officer Raúl Rodríguez

(His experience was credited as what was seen at the crime scene).

-At the scene of the crime, did you find any element that caught your attention and that you seized to present to the prosecution?
-Yes, I kidnapped a key, a chain, a pillow, and a flashlight.
-First of all, let's talk about the little chain found; where did you find it?
-I found her fallen on the floor next to the victim's body lying on the bed.
-What was the chain like?
-It was a silver-plated chain with two medals with initials on them.
-If I show you that little chain, would you recognize it?

(I allow your Honor to show the witness the evidence marked as A2, and I proceed to show it to my adversary, and then I show it to the witness).

-Do you recognize this evidence?
-Yes, I recognize her.
-Why do you recognize her?
-Because it was enveloped, it has the label and the date of the crime, plus there is my signature.
-Tell us about the chain, then; what are the initials on it?
-The initials are JM.
-Why did you lift it?
-Because the place in which they were found seemed suspicious to me, and I also noticed that it was broken, which gave me the indication that there was a possible struggle between the victim and the accused and that they already knew each other.
-What information were you able to obtain from the preliminary investigation you conducted? Who was the owner of that chain for you?
-From the inquiries I made with witnesses and neighbors of the victim, Priscila, I was able to determine that she had a partner or close friend named Juan Manuel. That is why I contacted the prosecutor's office to request his arrest.

(End of the introduction of the material evidence of the initialed chain)

-You also told me that you found a bunch of keys at the crime scene.

(I may proceed to exhibit the evidence or ask for certain details of the evidence; once the accreditation steps linking the witness to the evidence have been completed, I ask again for permission to show the evidence marked A4).

-Where did you find these keys?
-I found them on the top step of the staircase leading to the room where the victim's body was found.

-And did you do anything with those keys?
-Yes, before enveloping it with gloves, of course, I tried to see if the keys opened any of the doors of the house.
-And what did you discover?
-I discovered that two of the five keys on the key ring unlocked the doors to the house.
-When you entered, were the doors of the dwelling open or closed?
-When I arrived, the front door was locked with the key on the inside. What we also found was the garage door open.
-Could this key have been used to enter the house?
-Yes.

(From this point, I can move on to other sections of the factual proposition related to authorship).

-Was it possible to determine to whom the keys belonged?
-The DNA trace matched that of the defendant.

(It is advisable to end the interrogation at the strongest part, such as this one).

Next, the prosecution asks your honor to incorporate evidence A1 and A2 into evidence at trial.

Defense counter-examination of police officer Raul Rodriguez through suggestive questions *(Defense strategy: to prove the innocence of his client by alleging prejudice on the part of his defendants and alleging the possibility of another guilty party).*

-Let's talk about the little chain you talked about with the prosecutor. Was that little chain broken at the time it was found?
-Yes.
-Did you find it on the floor next to the victim's feet?
-That's right.
-And the initials you saw on the chain were JM's?
-Yes.
-And from those initials and your investigations, you determined that the chain belonged to Juan Manuel?
-Yes.
-Didn't that little chain have a last name or date of birth?
-That's right, I didn't have one.
-After finding that little chain, do I ask the prosecutor to arrest my client
-Yes.
-When you met with my client, he denied any knowledge of this chain.
-Yes.
-My client also mentioned to him that the victim had a brother with the same initials, Juan Molina.
-Yes.
-However, you did not request his arrest or proceed to investigate him?

-No, I didn't.
-No further questions.

(At this point, the defense cross-examines on the evidence marked A3, the keys).

-Now let's talk about the keys; you said that these keys were found on the last step of the staircase.
-That's right.
-Stairs leading to the room where the victim's body was found.
-Yes.
-He said that the key ring had five keys, of which only two opened the doors of Priscila's house.
-Yes.
-Keys were working properly?
-Yes.
-When you did the preliminary investigation, did you discover that the rest of the keys did not belong to the house?
-Yes.
-He was also unable to determine to whom the keys belonged.
-Yes.
-What he did discover, was it that other people had the keys to Priscila's house?
-That's right.
-One was the mother?
-Yes.
-And the other was the victim's brother.
-Yes.
-Juan Molina, right?
-That's right.
When interviewing my client's co-workers, was I able to collect relevant information?
-Yes.
-And those co-workers told him that my assistant had lost his keys several days before.

(The prosecution could object that the information sought is hearsay, assuming the objection does not proceed).

-That's right.
-At the time of the interview with my client, he told him that he had seen those keys on the desk of one of his colleagues.
-Yes, maybe.
-And that this partner was Juan Molina.
-Maybe I don't remember very well.
-And that partner is also the victim's brother.
-Yes, it is the brother.

(I terminate the interrogation)

Resolution of the example

From these examples, it can be seen that there is some doubt that the evidence does not lead to linking Juan Manuel as the perpetrator of the crime, so there may be another suspect. It can be seen how the two pieces of evidence found bring great doubt about their correspondence with the accused, but they also seek to attack the work of the witness and his prejudice from which he directed all his investigation, seeking to incriminate Juan Manuel.

HOW SHOULD YOU ASK TO A HOSTILE WITNESS?

STRATEGIES TO TURN HOSTILITY INTO OPPORTUNITY!

"There is nothing worse for your adversary than to know your light in full darkness."

DH

What is a hostile witness?

We understand a hostile witness to be one who expresses a position contrary to that of the lawyer who is cross-examining him or her. The motives behind this hostility can vary widely, but crucially, if the trial lawyer has done a solid job of research beforehand, he or she will likely have identified these motives. This will enable him or her to strategically plan how to conduct the direct or cross-examination of that witness.

However, on some occasions, hostility may arise surprisingly during the oral trial, presenting an additional challenge. In such situations, oral litigation techniques do not always provide precise guidelines on how to approach these hostile witnesses. Therefore, the lawyer's adaptability and skill become critical to successfully handle these unforeseen situations in court.

Techniques for successfully dealing with hostile witnesses

> 📢 Turn *witness hostility into an opportunity to strengthen your case!*

In oral litigation, facing a hostile witness is a challenge that requires a well-thought-out strategy. These situations are usually divided into two main scenarios.

The first occurs during cross-examination when we are questioning a witness sympathetic to our adversary's theory. Generally, we know that this witness is likely to show resistance.

In most cases, the witness expects us to question his or her credibility or testimony. Here, it is essential to remember that counsel must be prepared for this hostility. **Second, the attorney must understand that the witness, presented by the adversary, may also show hostility.**

However, with proper planning, the attorney can successfully approach a hostile witness. This involves a strategy that goes beyond questioning credibility. It involves skillfully navigating through challenging responses and remaining calm.

When confronted with a witness who surprisingly displays hostility during oral argument, it is essential for the trial lawyer to know how to approach this situation strategically. Hostility can manifest itself in a variety of ways, and it is the attorney's responsibility to plan the appropriate approach.

Two possible approaches:

1. Control and intimidating posture

In some cases, it may be effective to maintain control and an intimidating posture toward the hostile witness. This involves marking the attorney's authority and setting clear boundaries.

2. Disarming the witness

A less conventional but effective strategy is to try to disarm the hostile witness. Here, the attorney seeks to demonstrate that he or she is in search of the truth and is not looking for a confrontation. Begin by asking questions on subjects in which the witness is comfortable and by addressing issues in which the witness does not have to assume any of the positions taken by the parties, thus seeking to steer the witness toward an unbiased attitude.

The importance of starting with neutrality

When beginning the cross-examination, it is critical to address neutral issues so that the witness is no longer on the defensive. Often, the witness is not completely biased, and the attorney can establish rapport through close-ended questions.

Use leading questions

If the witness continues to be hostile, the attorney can use suggestive rather than close-ended questions. This approach can help ease the tension and allow the cross-examination to continue more smoothly.

Maintain unwavering professionalism

Regardless of the approach chosen, it is imperative that the attorney maintain a high level of professionalism at all times. The witness may show hostility, but the attorney should never respond in kind. Mistreatment, inappropriate words, or any conduct that increases the witness' discomfort should be avoided at all times.

Ultimately, the key is to adapt your approach according to the behavior of the witness while always maintaining ethics and respect. Litigation is an art that requires mastery of both strategy and demeanor.

When is it appropriate for the trial lawyer to use leading questions?

The role of the trial lawyer goes beyond asking leading questions. Each interrogation, whether direct or cross-examination, must be carefully planned in light of the overall strategy of the case. The priority is not simply to prove a witness's lack of credibility but rather to achieve the objectives set forth in the theory of the case.

Before cross-examining a witness, it is essential to stop and assess whether this action will effectively contribute to the strategy. Can the witness's testimony be effectively challenged? Are there obvious contradictions in the witness's statement or material evidence to support our argument? These are key questions.

The decision to cross-examine – or not – will depend on the specific strategy of the litigator in each case. Successful litigation requires a strategic approach, where each step is aligned with the theory of the case and the desired objectives.

Cross-examination, a crucial stage in the oral trial, requires a thematic and selective strategy.

Bearing in mind, of course, that strategy is essential. In cross-examination or indirect examination, we must abandon the chronological sequence and opt for a thematic approach. The trial lawyer's goal is to elicit selective information to support our narrative; we do not seek to provide complete information, unlike direct examination. Our goal is to extract key facts to tell the part of the story that supports our position.

When confronting a hostile witness, after attempting to calm his or her demeanor, we can question his or her credibility. This could involve pointing out that the witness has withheld information, has ties to the parties involved, harbors enmity toward our client, or is influenced by bias toward one of the parties involved. We can also examine the conditions that affect his or her perception.

Regardless of the reason behind our approach, it is essential that the lawyer maintains a decisive posture and conveys confidence through his or her body language. Staring the witness in the eye, maintaining a firm posture, and a convincing tone of voice are key elements.

When we pose leading questions, the change in intonation from interrogation to affirmation strengthens our credibility with the judge. Skillfully executed cross-examination can be a powerful tool in the search for truth in the judicial process.

The importance of the rhythm of questions and answers at trial

Undoubtedly, the pace of response and questioning play a critical role in the oral litigation process. When approaching a witness, the strategy must be clear and tailored to our objectives.

To achieve automatic responses and avoid giving the witness time to think, it is crucial to maintain a rapid pace of questioning. This involves a smooth transition between topics and, often, silence once the desired answer is obtained.

On the other hand, if the objective is to gain the confidence of the witness, it is necessary to give him/her time to reflect on the questions. In this case, the pace of the questions should be slower at first and gradually accelerate, especially when the key point of the interrogation is reached. In situations where an initially sympathetic witness becomes hostile, it is essential to remember that we are not obliged to prove the motives behind this change in behavior. Our focus should be on the witness's testimony in the current context.

Even when faced with a hostile witness who has not been subpoenaed by our opposing party, it is important to subpoena the witness to testify at trial and conduct direct examination. Adversarial testimony can reveal valuable information for our case.

Consequently, proper management of the pace of response and questioning is essential to achieve our objectives in oral litigation and to adapt to the different situations that may arise at trial.

Undoubtedly, interacting with a hostile witness is a challenge in the litigation process. Here, step by step, I will guide you to approach this situation with professionalism and strategy.

1. Identification of the hostile witness

During direct examination, it is crucial to recognize when a witness is hostile or evasive. This is manifested when he or she evades questions or shows reticence.

2. Establish the basis

Initially, use open-ended questions to expose the hostility of the witness. Ask for details with questions such as "what," "how," "when," "where," and "who."

3. Request permission

When you have made the hostility clear, ask the court for permission to treat the witness as a "hostile witness." This change allows you to move from direct examination to cross-examination, where you can use leading questions.

4. Control of the counter-examination

In cross-examination, you provide the information and guide the witness's answers. This gives you greater control over the cross-examination. You ask leading questions to elicit a yes or no answer from the witness.

Open questions	Suggestive questions
How many people were in the house?	*There were five people in the house.*
Was Emma present?	*Emma was present*
At five o'clock in the afternoon, was the defendant present?	*At five o'clock in the afternoon, Emma opened the door to the defendant.*

5. Impress the judge and court

Your professional handling of a hostile witness reflects your knowledge of procedural rules and litigation techniques. It shows that you have a solid plan and are committed despite the difficulties.

6. Maintain firmness

When faced with a witness who denies answers, stay calm and stick to your plan. Avoid being provoked and effectively seek ways to obtain information.

7. Refreshing memory and contradiction

Use previous statements of the witness to refresh his or her memory or to evidence contradictions. This strategy is valuable in establishing the truth.

8. Continuous adaptation

If the witness changes his or her attitude upon realizing that you possess information, adjust your approach accordingly.

Dealing with a hostile witness requires decisiveness, skill, and professionalism. Maintain your composure and be strategic in your approach, demonstrating your ability and leadership as a trial lawyer.

Thus, handling a hostile witness at trial is a challenge that requires skill and strategy on the part of the trial lawyer. Identifying the signs of hostility, laying the groundwork with open-ended questions, and asking the court to allow the witness to be treated as hostile are crucial steps in this process.

Also, the transition from direct examination to cross-examination is critical to gaining control over the testimony and showing professionalism in court. In addition, the presentation of prior statements can be an effective tool to refresh the witness's memory or demonstrate contradictions.

At all times, the lawyer must maintain composure, avoid provocation, and follow a strategic plan. The ultimate goal is to present a strong and convincing case to the court, demonstrating mastery of procedural rules and litigation techniques.

PROFESSIONAL ADVICE

★ *"Being a professional litigator, you don't have to fear the unexpected because that word has ceased to exist for you."*

- Deborah Huczek

THE PERFORMANCE OF THE JUDGE IN THE ADVERSARIAL ACCUSATORY SYSTEM

ADMINISTRATOR AND GUARDIAN OF JUSTICE

Oral litigation maxim 9: You cannot be both judge and party.

The judge shall remain strictly outside the dispute in every act and intervention in order to preserve his impartiality.

A judge is said to be a judge who, as a representative of one of the powers of the State, has among his duties that of imparting justice, interpreting what the law says and how it applies to the particular case.

The judge is, in the end, the one who explains the law to us, the lawful ones. He interprets it, nourishes himself with its spirit, subsumes it to the case, and gives it meaning. The judge puts the law into action.

However, experience teaches us that when faced with the same or similar cases, judges tend to vary their interpretation if we compare what other judges decide and even what the same judge decides in different periods of time.

Therefore, we could conclude that the law does not say the same thing to all judges, and that is why it is not applied in the same way.

Not to mention those cases that were decided by a collegiate court, where 3 judges participated in the same trial, heard the witnesses say the same words and yet came to different conclusions.

That is why we lawyers usually tell our clients that: ***"everything depends on the case,"*** and with that, we avoid explaining in depth how uncertain it is to navigate in this legal world, where we can never or very rarely anticipate a result.

In affirming the foregoing, oral litigation contributes greatly to this uncertainty, since it offers us various ways of presenting the case to the judge, with the purpose of persuading him and ultimately establishing that the law is in our favor. In terms of probabilities, it is undeniable that a good litigator will have more chances of obtaining favorable results than one who is not.

As true as it is that even if you are the best litigator in the world, you must remember that the final decision does not belong to you.

A long time ago, we understood that although the judge and justice have the same etymological roots, they do not mean the same thing; therefore, we could face an unjust result even if the trial was conducted by a judge.

Without going deeper into these concepts, the truth is that justice is also a term with a subjective scope and, therefore, variable for each person at each time and place. Is this why practicing law is so complex and exciting at the same time?

Returning to the subject, throughout this chapter, I intend to address some main aspects related to the role of judges and their relationship with oral litigation.

However, before doing so, I would like to express a few words in favor of those who have the burden of settling other people's disputes, whether it may result in a sanction of patrimonial content, order the life of a broken or dysfunctional family, establish pecuniary obligations, restore the contact of parents with their children, resolve whether a person should pay for what he did by sending him to prison, and so many other issues.

Delivering justice must be one of the most difficult tasks to perform; the responsibility is too great, and the consequences of their mistakes are practically indelible.

Judges break with their decisions and the life plans of others by establishing what they consider to be fair, according to their interpretation of the law.

It is really complex to be in the judge's shoes.

I am saddened that this function has been so discredited, and for this reason, I would also like to emphasize the importance of its work since it seeks to balance the different social relationships.

I humbly hope to collaborate in some way and improve the lawyer-judge relationship and vice versa. That we can see role and case from the other's point of view, who should not be our adversary at all since we have both been imbued with a spirit of justice, which is what ultimately led us to choose this profession among so many existing ones.

My objective with regard to the judicial function is to bring another view that is useful when managing the process and the techniques deployed by the litigants in action.

On the other hand, and in order to contribute to these objectives, I consider it essential and urgent to promote certain legislative reforms. I believe that a reform is urgent and necessary, at least in Argentina, regarding the procedure established for the nomination and selection of judges. In this sense, I believe that it could contribute to a better justice system to require those who intend to become judges to have practiced the litigation profession for at least 10 years prior to their nomination. This could really improve the performance of such an essential public function and, therefore, increase the confidence of individuals.

Role of the judge and accusatory system

The adversarial system is a model of justice that has been consolidated in several Latin American countries in recent years. This system seeks to guarantee a fair and transparent trial by giving an active role to the parties involved in the criminal process, such as prosecutors, defense attorneys, and, of course, judges.

The role of the judge in the adversarial process is critical to ensuring the fairness and equity inherent in a fair trial. **In this system, the judge serves as an impartial arbiter, overseeing the process, applying the relevant laws, and making impartial decisions based on the evidence presented by the opposing parties.**

One of the judge's primary functions is to ensure that the trial is conducted in accordance with court rules and legal principles.

In this context, the judge has the responsibility to enforce procedural rules, ensuring that both parties have an equal opportunity to present their cases, that evidence is properly admitted, and that legal arguments are duly considered.

> **THE JUDGE ensures the fairness and the orderly execution of the trial.**

The judge also assumes responsibility for ruling on legal issues that may arise during the trial. This area ranges from the interpretation and application of laws to determining the relevance of evidence and making decisions on procedural matters. That is, the judge may decide on the admissibility of certain evidence or witness testimony based on the applicable rules of evidence and legal principles.

In addition to his or her procedural and legal duties, the judge also has a responsibility to ensure that the trial is conducted with respect for the fundamental principles of justice and fairness.

This involves ensuring respectful treatment of all participants, preventing undue influence or prejudice that could affect the process, and safeguarding the defendant's right to a fair trial.

Litigation skills. The link with justice

Litigation skills are not merely a set of public speaking or dramatic acting techniques. Rather, they are presented as a fundamental strategic tool for judges, prosecutors, defense attorneys, and lawyers in general who participate in an adversarial system. These skills enable legal professionals to understand

and apply procedural rules in the context of an actual oral trial, where strategy, logic, and argumentation are crucial.

One of the fundamental aspects that demonstrate the relationship between litigation and effective trial management occurs primarily at the evidentiary stage during the development of the trial, specifically when litigants execute the techniques of examination and cross-examination. Without a thorough understanding of how these stages of the trial are conducted or a lack of a thorough understanding of the litigants' theory of the case, judges may have difficulty assessing the credibility of witnesses, determining the relevance of evidence, and making critical decisions.

For example, the ability to conduct effective cross-examination is essential to obtaining accurate and complete information from a witness. If a judge does not understand the dynamics of cross-examination, he or she could miss valuable information that should influence his or her final decision.

On the other hand, within the skills of litigation, an important factor is the construction of a solid case theory. We know that the theory of the case is the logical structure that guides the strategy of each litigant at trial. Here, judges play a key role, as they must evaluate and understand the parties' theories in order to make decisions that are more in line with the law.

If a judge does not possess a thorough knowledge of litigation skills, it is likely that he or she will not be able to fully appreciate the theory of the case presented by each party. This can lead to misinterpretations or misguided decisions and, in the worst case, injustice.

The road to effective justice

The relationship between litigation skills
and the role of judges in the system
the adversarial system is undeniable.

A judge well prepared in these skills is better equipped to understand and apply procedural rules in a real trial context. Knowledge of the dynamics of litigation, the process of examination and cross-examination, the construction of theories of the case, and an understanding of the reality of trial are essential elements of an effective justice system.

In other words, litigation and the foundations of due process comprise two indivisible aspects of the adversarial system. A judge who does not understand litigation skills limits his or her ability to properly apply procedural rules and ultimately stands in the way of genuine and effective justice in our society.

The Role of Judges in the Adversarial Accusatory Process

The role of the judge in the adversarial process

- *It is in charge of arbitrating the process in an impartial manner so that the parties have equal opportunities.*
- *It must protect the fundamental rights of all parties.*
- *Make decisions based on the law, not personal bias.*
- *It ensures that the principle of presumption of innocence is respected.*
- *He shall control the proceedings and ensure the maintenance of order in the courtroom.*
- *It must issue a sentence, ensuring that it is fair and in accordance with the law.*
- *It is responsible for ensuring confidence in the system.*

One of the most essential roles of a judge in the adversarial system is to be an impartial arbiter. This means that the judge must ensure that both sides have the opportunity to present their arguments and evidence without any bias. To achieve this, the judge must make impartial decisions on objections, evidence, and other procedural issues.

The judge -must- hear and consider the arguments of both parties before making a decision. This impartiality is crucial to maintain the integrity of the process and to ensure that all parties are treated fairly.

➢ ***Guaranteeing fundamental rights***

Judges play a fundamental role in protecting the fundamental rights of all parties involved in the judicial process. This includes rights such as the right to a fair trial, the right to counsel, the right to be free from unlawful interrogation or searches, and many others. **Judges have the responsibility to ensure that these rights are respected and protected at all times.**

➢ ***Decision making***

Judges must also make a number of decisions throughout the judicial process. This may include decisions on the admissibility of evidence, requests for change of venue, rulings, and other matters. Decisions made by a judge can have a significant impact on the outcome of a case.

However, when violations of these rights occur, judges must take steps to remedy the situation. This may include the exclusion of illegally obtained evidence, the reversal of a conviction, or a mistrial. Therefore, a judge's decisions must be based on the law and not on personal bias.

➢ ***Presumption of innocence***

A key principle of the adversarial system is the presumption of innocence. This means that a person accused of a crime is considered innocent until proven guilty beyond a reasonable doubt. Judges have the responsibility to ensure that this principle is respected at all times.

In practice, this means that judges must instruct the jury on the presumption of innocence and on the standard of proof necessary to convict someone. They must also avoid making statements or taking actions that suggest they are prejudiced about the defendant's guilt or innocence.

➢ ***Judgment control***

The judge is also responsible for controlling the course of the trial. This includes managing the presentation of evidence, ruling on objections, and resolving disputes between the parties. The judge has the authority to maintain order in the courtroom and ensure that the trial is conducted efficiently and fairly.

In addition to the above, the judge may pass sentence after a guilty verdict, imposing the appropriate penalty according to the law and the circumstances of the case. It is necessary that this sentence complies with legal principles and ensures that the penalty is fair and proportionate.

➢ ***The importance of impartiality***

One of the greatest challenges facing judges in an adversarial system is maintaining their impartiality. Often, court cases involve emotional issues and intense conflicts between the parties. Judges must strive not to take sides and treat all parties fairly. And to comply with this, judges may be excluded from cases in which they have a conflict of interest or where they have obvious biases. **Independence and impartiality are essential to public confidence in the justice system.**

The judge, in his or her position as an administrator of justice, cannot afford to be a mere observer of litigation. His or her ability to make informed decisions and understand procedural rules depends on his or her deep understanding of the dynamics of litigation. Litigation is not simply a set of techniques; it is the bridge between criminal procedural theory and the reality of trial. By embracing litigation, the judge strengthens his or her ability to deliver justice in tune with the values and needs of society.

PROFESSIONAL ADVICE

★ *Litigants must demonstrate to the judge commitment to the case and respect for his or her office.*

★ *Judges must respect the work of litigants at trial.*

DEMOCRATIZING JUSTICE: BENEFITS OF LITIGATING BEFORE A POPULAR JURY

"History has shown that it is jurors who can fulfill the guarantee of impartiality better than anyone else, because they have no offices to defend and no positions to climb to."

Déborah Huczek

In the current context, where fairness in justice has become an imperative demand, jury trials represent a significant revolution. This method of trial not only involves citizens actively in the decisions of the Judiciary but also offers a series of benefits that transform the judicial dynamics.

To go to the concrete level, in the province of Buenos Aires -and with similarities to the classic format seen in Hollywood movies- jury trials are here to stay. Lawyers from both sides present their arguments before a jury of 12 citizens, replicating the essence of the U.S. judicial system.

The implementation of this model has also spread to the Federal Capital and provinces such as Mendoza, where landmark cases, such as the "cat man" -a man who killed his mother and aunt - have been tried with a jury that reflects gender parity.

➢ **Ensuring impartiality: A fundamental role of the people's jury.**

Citizen participation seeks to ensure impartiality, as jurors – outside of government functions – strive to minimize the influence of outside information. Although the total absence of "contamination" is difficult, the magistrate's instructions direct jurors to base their decisions solely on the evidence presented during the trial.

Thus, each juror -without access to the record and unaware of prior testimony- guarantees a trial based on proven facts and avoids conjecture or supposition. This approach, in addition to supporting due process, also strengthens the impartiality of the verdict.

Moreover, citizens, by committing to their role as jurors in a trial, have demonstrated their ability to efficiently assume this commitment. The efficiency and responsibility with which they fulfill their functions underscores the viability and acceptance of this participatory system.

➢ **A safeguard for the accused when being judged by his peers.**

To continue, it is necessary to point out that trial by jury acts as a safeguard for the accused since it guarantees that he will be judged by ordinary citizens... by his peers.

It is also important to note that the victim cannot request this type of trial, and the defendant, through his defense attorney, is obliged to waive this option. Likewise, the accused has the right not to testify if he so chooses.

In Argentina, for example, there are relevant cases that illustrate the success of this system, from the acquittal of Guillermo Alberto Barros for homicide to the conviction of Fernando Farré for femicide. These cases underline the effectiveness and capacity of the jury to evaluate and decide impartially.

Among the advantages and benefits of a trial by jury are publicity, immediacy, and transparency, which are essential elements to guarantee an efficient judicial process. The trial by a popular jury offers additional advantages by highlighting the impartiality of persons outside the case, with no interest in the outcome. Free from political or popular pressures, jurors immerse themselves in days of testimony and expert testimony, evaluating the lawyers' conclusions to determine who is right, applying common sense. This modality maximizes time efficiency, meeting the popular clamor for prompt and effective justice, guaranteeing a verdict within a reasonable period of time.

Strengthening judicial effectiveness to restore faith in the judiciary

> *The preparation and execution of your strategy is critical to avoid potential misunderstandings and to ensure a coherent and convincing presentation to the jury.*

Litigating before a popular jury represents a great advantage in the dynamics of the oral trial. The litigant, in addition to presenting his case before professional judges – or judges of law – will also do so before citizens who will assume the role of judges of fact. And these, unlike the former, are more focused on knowing how the facts happened. They will look for clear answers and solid evidence to help them decide in the most impartial and favorable way possible; their loyalty to the judicial process is intrinsically linked to the search for the truth, and if the facts that are the object of the accusation are not reliably proven, they will opt for acquittal without complications. They do not seek to distort or manipulate the law to convict for the sake of conviction.

That is why lawyers should use simple language, avoiding technicalities that may generate confusion. In addition, it is essential that they develop the new skills of the litigator that we discuss throughout this book -leader, strategist, investigator, and storyteller-; this will allow them, in turn, to carry out a powerfully effective communication where oratory, the ability to connect with the audience and the application of Non-Verbal Communication (NVC) play a crucial role. The ability to convey information in a clear and persuasive manner then becomes transcendental, as it is these skills that will give the jury a real basis for an informed decision.

This is why strategic litigation is so important to the success of the lawyer and the delivery of justice because a jury will not tolerate errors that compromise the integrity of the case. In other words, the lawyer must know how to present the evidence effectively and, in addition, make sure that key information is not lost in the attempt to translate it into language accessible to the jurors.

At this point, it is vital to emphasize that the implementation of jury trials and the oral and public hearing system demands constant training of lawyers. Beyond mastery of law and jurisprudence, they must be prepared to demonstrate their theory during the trial. This entails developing research skills and assuming the guidance of collaborators; it is also essential that they be trained in oral litigation techniques, public speaking, and non-verbal communication.

The trial system, while comprehensive, must adapt to emerging demands. For example, consideration could be given to modifying the number of votes required to find the defendant guilty, requiring unanimity instead of a majority, as is currently the case in some jurisdictions. This preserves the principle of innocence, ensuring that no one is convicted without absolute certainty of guilt. Another aspect that needs to be studied in greater depth is the method of introducing evidence, requiring more complete regulations. In addition, the right of lawyers to interview witnesses without criminal charges must be guaranteed, and methods must be regulated to ensure results, such as recording or notarization of interviews.

As we can see, citizen participation in the trial of their peers ensures the effectiveness of the judicial system, restores confidence in justice, and gives the community the responsibility to resolve cases with seriousness and common sense, aspects often absent in many magistrates.

In short, we must train ourselves to litigate in front of the judges of the facts because they are committed to discovering the truth.

CONCLUSIONS

Reflection on the importance of Oral Litigation:

Why mastering it is vital in every lawyer's career?

This compendium of oral litigation techniques has been a journey through the various essential skills that make up the potential of every successful litigator. From developing self-leadership to mastery in strategy to thorough research and storytelling skills, this book has explored the DH Method, i.e., the formula for winning and shining in the competitive world of oral litigation.

In each chapter, we have broken down the litigation techniques that correspond to the various stages of the oral trial, where the lawyer's skills are put to the test in a public and dynamic manner. Mastery of these techniques and stages of the oral trial thus becomes a crucial element for the litigator seeking to present sound arguments and persuade the court of the validity of his or her position.

Now, why do I tell you that mastering oral litigation is vital to the success of your professional career?

Well, because in addition to the fact that it has been gaining more and more ground in the justice systems of Latin America, oral litigation is the act of humanizing the search for justice, of putting faces and emotions at the center of the dispute, as well as delving into the facts and their causes, which makes it more equitable and competent in the application of the law.

Beyond the acrimony of files and documents, litigation uses every word spoken and every gesture to build a story that turns the parties involved into complex characters with motivations, conflicts, and rights holders. This implies that in order to find the best solution, a scenario where persuasion reaches its maximum expression must be constructed.

Thus, the litigator needs to be able to tell the audience what happened and why, who the people involved are, and how, when, and where it happened. And he must do so in such a way that his speech can take his listeners through an emotional journey that allows them to feel the relevance and veracity of his arguments.

For as we saw throughout this book that, in a courtroom, we are not just presenting facts; we are telling stories, stories that must resonate in the court's consciousness.

Another reason to improve or learn litigation techniques is that in the dynamics of oral litigation, there are no second chances since it is a real-time act that requires – on the part of the litigant – mental agility and the ability to act according to the objectives. That is, knowing how to object and respond effectively to objections, cross-examine with dexterity, and know how to handle hostile witnesses or any other unthinkable situations while adjusting the strategy in the process.

Mastering oral litigation involves knowing the law and having the skill to apply it in the heat of the moment, anticipating and adapting to the complexities of trial.

If a lawyer does not know how to communicate effectively, even if he or she has very good arguments in his or her repertoire, he or she loses points in the legal dispute. Knowing the rules of litigation, as well as how to communicate and persuade audiences, is notoriously essential to building credibility. The way we present the case (showing the deep knowledge we have of it) and the confidence and assurance we project all will be part of the perception that the jury and the judge will have about the validity of our arguments.

Oral litigation, then, will connect legal knowledge with real, concrete action in the courtroom. Making law and justice come alive, humanized, and reliably presented to society.

A litigator who exercises leadership and masters the techniques of oral litigation, in addition to being distinguished by his or her skill in legal knowledge, is also distinguished by his or her ability to inspire and guide others, whether it be his or her client, his or her team or third parties with decision-making power. We have underscored the importance of cultivating relationships based on trust and transparency, recognizing that collaboration is key in the pursuit of justice.

The adversarial system focuses on the search for truth and impartiality and demands a litigator who is prepared, ethical, and capable of adapting to a dynamic environment.

It is worth saying that this process, with its principles of orality, publicity, immediacy, contradiction, simplicity, celerity, and informalization, stands then as the legal framework that supports and enhances the skills of the litigant at the same time as it demands its existence.

Ultimately, the DH method not only provides detailed guidance for the litigator committed to his or her professional success but also advocates a holistic approach that transcends the boundaries of the courtroom. Being a leading litigator is more than merely a theoretical skill; it is a commitment to integrity, ethics, and service to justice.

At this point, I have encouraged you to discover, demonstrate, and tell your own story on the courtroom stage (and off) to become an expert storyteller who, through persuasion and consistency, wins the minds and hearts of decision-makers.

So, as you close this book, I invite you to take with you not only the techniques and strategies you have learned but also the conviction that you are capable of leading with integrity and excellence in every case you undertake. This book is your traveling companion on the wonderful journey to professional success and personal fulfillment in the controversial and wonderful field of oral litigation.

Go forth, litigator; the courtroom is yours to conquer!

BIBLIOGRAPHIC REFERENCES

BAYTELMAN, A., & DUCE J., M. (2004). *Criminal Litigation. Oral trial and evidence.* Universidad Diego Portales. Santiago, Chile: 1st edition.

HUCZEK, D. (Ed.). (2020). Orality and civil process. *Various authors. Rubinzal - Culzoni Editores. Buenos Aires: 1st edition.*

JAUCHEN, E. (2015). Criminal Procedure. *Rubinzal - Culzoni Editores. Buenos Aires.*

LORENZO, L. (2015). *Litigation Manual. Litigation and adversarial criminal prosecution collection.* Ediciones Didot. Buenos Aires: 1st edition.

MAXWELL, J. C. (2015). *Intentional living.* Center Street. New York: 1st edition.

MORENO HOLMAN, L. (2013). *Case Theory. Litigation and Adversarial Criminal Prosecution Collection.* Ediciones Didot. Buenos Aires: 1st edition.

RODRIGUEZ VÁZQUEZ, M. Á. (2013). *Cassation and the right to appeal in the accusatory system.* Universidad Autónoma de México, Instituto de Investigaciones Jurídicas: 1st edition.

www.ingramcontent.com/pod-product-compliance
Lightning Source LLC
LaVergne TN
LVHW060212210926
848481LV00008B/2703